THE GREAT BELONGING

THE GREAT BELONGING

How Loneliness Leads
Us to Each Other

Charlotte Donlon

 Broadleaf Books

Minneapolis

THE GREAT BELONGING
How Loneliness Leads Us to Each Other

"Flood: Years of Solitude" from *Bad Alchemy* by Dionisio D. Martínez. Copyright © 1995 by Dionisio D. Martínez. Used by permission of W. W. Norton & Company, Inc.

Portions of chapter 42 were first published in "The Mockingbird Blog," https://mbird.com/.

The names of some of the people in this book have been changed to protect their identities.

Unless otherwise noted, scripture quotations are from the New Revised Standard Version of the Bible, copyright © 1989 by the Division of Christian Education of the National Council of Churches of Christ in the USA and used by permission. All rights reserved.

Cover design and artwork: Cindy Laun

Print ISBN: 978-1-5064-6196-0
eBook ISBN: 978-1-5064-6197-7

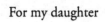
For my daughter

Contents

Part I
Belonging to Ourselves

Part II
Belonging to Each Other

Part III
Belonging to Our Places

Part IV
Belonging through Art

Part V
Belonging to God

Foreword

The book you are holding does not aim to cure your loneliness. Instead, *The Great Belonging* addresses loneliness as a companion. As you would with any companion, *The Great Belonging* inquires into loneliness—into loneliness's history, and habits, and fears. And in the company of *The Great Belonging*'s fearless and smart author, Charlotte Donlon, we, the readers, are allowed to indulge our interest in loneliness. I, for one, am interested in both senses of the term. I am curious about loneliness, and I am involved in loneliness, affected by loneliness, implicated in loneliness. I am companioned by it; I want to get to know it better.

Because loneliness touches the whole of life, *The Great Belonging*'s inquiry into loneliness becomes also a straightforwardly fascinating inquiry into lighthouses, body temperature, sex, Georgia O'Keeffe's *Trees in Autumn,* death, prayer, illness, and the communion of saints. One of Donlon's key insights is that loneliness can open us up to ourselves and to the world—to other people, to poetry, to a tree. If you look back to the table of contents, you'll see that the book is divided into five sections. *The Great*

Belonging does not argue that those five—ourselves, others, art, places, and God—are merely antidotes to loneliness, though to be sure sometimes a painting, a friend, or the God we meet in the psalter does provide succor in our loneliness. Rather, *The Great Belonging* suggests that, like all my other companions, loneliness introduces me to people I wouldn't have met on my own, and to places I wouldn't have found. And loneliness helps me see things in familiar books or paintings or parks that I wouldn't have seen without loneliness's tutelage. Our belonging to ourselves, to each other, to God—all those belongings can shush loneliness when she starts exaggerating and telling us tales. But equally, it is often through and with loneliness that we find our many other manifold belongings.

Donlon is not someone you'd stereotype as lonely. She's married. She has two pretty cool kids. She is engaged at her church. But she has always known loneliness, which suggests that loneliness is quite subtle. Loneliness is an indiscriminate visitor. She will not pass you by simply because you have a husband or a group of friends. Reading this book has helped me name something in my own life: I live alone and I often work alone, but I rarely feel lonely when alone. Rather, some of my loneliest lonesome strikes when I am with my best friend. When I am with her, I sense the stern reality that we are ultimately always separate from one another—we are always removed from others, even from those we know best and cherish most intimately. Donlon's insistence on framing loneliness as something that might come to us all is helping me see more clearly that loneliness is not principally a feeling—and it's certainly not principally a feeling that only afflicts the widow or the divorcee. Rather, loneliness is a right response—an insightful response—to the ways intimacy and distance are insistently threaded together in all our lives.

I hope you and your loneliness will love this book as much as I do, and that the friendship between the two of you will be enriched by what you find in these pages.

—Lauren F. Winner, author of *Wearing God* and *Still: Notes on a Mid-Faith Crisis*

Introduction

Sometimes I wonder if loneliness resides in an extra, secret organ within the body—maybe the size of a plum, a storehouse of dense alienation hidden deep within us. I wonder if God knew we'd need a special place for our loneliness because we would have so much of it.

Everyone knows loneliness. Some may experience it more often. Some may find relief from it more quickly. Some may deny or avoid it. But I don't think any of us escapes its company entirely, and I'm no longer sure we should, though I spent many years trying to outrun loneliness and her cunning charms.

Indeed, being human requires a touch of loneliness. None of us will ever be fully known by another person. None of us will ever fully know or belong to another person or even to ourselves. This doesn't mean we should stop trying to know, be known, and belong. Rather, it means we can accept loneliness as a normal companion. We can inhabit a posture of curiosity when we recognize loneliness, and our responses to it, as part of the human condition.

We can wonder how our different forms of loneliness and our belongings are connected. While I was finishing this book, we were sheltering in place at home because of the global pandemic. Loneliness of all kinds spiked. Many of us began to wonder: Is my relationship with God affected by my inability to visit my best friend? Is my relationship with myself affected because I can't chat with neighbors at the grocery store? Is my relationship with my husband affected because we haven't been able to pray, worship, and take Communion at church? As everything begins to settle into different patterns, we can be curious about our new belongings. We can ask: Even though our familiar belongings are shifting and fading, what new belongings are being formed? What are some of the new ways I'm belonging to myself, others, and God?

We can dip our toes into the waters of loneliness and test the temperature. If it's comfortable—or bearable—we can dive on in. If the water seems too cold, we can wade in slowly, one step at a time. When we are submerged and ready, we can swim around and discover how it feels to move toward and through the deeper waters. And we can do all of this knowing we can climb out of the water at any time.

We can dive for the bright plastic circles of insight laying way down deep on the bottom. We can float on a raft and consider the shapes of the clouds in the blue sky above. We can notice who else is in the water with us. We can study their strokes and determine how long it takes them to get from where they are to where they want to be. And, together, we can make our way to whatever might be waiting for us.

Thank you for wading into the waters of loneliness with me. I pray we arrive on the other side full of hope.

Part I

BELONGING TO OURSELVES

1

The Opposite of Loneliness

If loneliness were placed on one side of a scale and belonging on the other, we might discover they carry the same weight. And if you ask people who struggle with loneliness if they would like to have a greater sense of belonging, most of them will respond with a hearty yes.

In her essay "The Opposite of Loneliness," young writer Marina Keegan writes:

We don't have a word for the opposite of loneliness, but if we did, I could say that's what I want in life. . . . It's not quite loving, and it's not quite a community; it's this feeling that there are people, an abundance of people, who are in this together. Who are on your team. When the check is paid, and you stay at the table. When it's four a.m., and no one goes to bed. That night with the guitar. That night we can't remember. That time we did, we went, we saw, we laughed, we felt.

Keegan didn't think there was a sufficient antonym for loneliness available in the English language. But I think *belonging* names what she's after in her evocative sentence-fragment list.

What is belonging? What does belonging mean in a practical, how-we-live-our-lives-in-the-real-world sense?

We can consider belonging through the lenses of self, others, and God. If we lived in a perfect world, we would always belong perfectly to ourselves, other people, and God. We would be sufficiently self-aware, have ideal relationships, and know God as we were designed to do so. But we don't live in a perfect world, and we face barriers to belonging at different times in our lives. Even when we are meaningfully connected to ourselves and to other people through our relationships and as members of groups, clubs, and faith organizations, we can still feel isolated and disquieted. It may seem like something is off, like everyone else belongs more. The insecurities we thought we'd let go of—we've worked so hard to be self-aware!—convince us we're imposters who really don't belong to anyone.

If we believe we are beloved children of God and united with Christ, then we trust our other belongings and unbelongings are wrapped up in a Great Belonging: this most significant and essential belonging in existence because of the love, grace, and mercy God lavishes on us. We can't belong to ourselves or others outside of our belonging to God. And the knowledge that God will never leave or forsake us is a kind of buoy as we navigate the waters of loneliness. I like to imagine these three belongings—to self, others, and God—as points on an inverted triangle, with belonging to God at the bottom point and belonging to self and belonging to others at the two equidistant higher points. I also envision various entryways to belonging dispersed along the three lines of the triangle. Our places and art are two such portals that can help us form closer bonds.

All of our belongings are connected and dependent on each other. But the belonging we have with God is the foundation. It is the rooted point that holds, supports, and sustains our additonal belongings. The psalmist says, "God claims Earth and everything in it. God claims World and all who live on it" (Ps 24:1 The Message). Knowing we are God's provides rest and comfort while making our other belongings possible. And while our belongings may not take away all of our loneliness, they might make it tamer, more tolerable.

If we pull the scale out again and place loneliness on one side and the Great Belonging on the other, will the two be equally balanced? Because of the weight and substance of the Great Belonging, I believe the scales will tip toward this more powerful force made possible by the love, grace, and mercy of God.

$$2$$

Core Loneliness

The Loneliness Project is an online gathering place in which people can share their personal stories of loneliness. Contributors submit stories anonymously, along with their first names (which may or may not be their real names) and their ages (which may or may not be their real ages). Those who send entries to the Loneliness Project are asked to complete some or all of the following four statements:

1. The last time I felt lonely was . . .
2. To me, loneliness means . . .
3. One of the first times I realized I was lonely was . . .
4. Tell me the story of the time you felt the most lonely.

Most of the responses are mundane yet distressing because of the participants' desperation. Those who shared their stories have lost a boyfriend or girlfriend; they have moved away from friends; their parents are terrible people. Situations along those lines highlight the deep sense of aloneness that many people experience, either chronically or else during specific seasons of life.

Reading the entries, I want to gather up all of the lonely people and put them into groups of three or four. I want to invite them in so they can talk, hang out, and celebrate the extraordinary and mundane events of life over glasses of wine or mugs of coffee.

But I also have to be honest: reading the submissions to this website displaces my own sense of disconnection. When I compare myself to the contributors' heartbroken voices, I realize that although I often feel lonely, I am not alone. I have a husband, two children, many supportive and loving extended family members, a few close friends, and several not-as-close friends. If I want to meet someone for coffee, or invite guests over for dinner, or touch or be touched, I have plenty of options.

My deepest sense of loneliness is what theologian Tom Varney calls "core loneliness." It's not simply situational feelings of rejection or isolation; rather, Varney says of core loneliness, "This kind of loneliness is more basic, more fundamental to our existence as human beings, and it is seldom discussed or even acknowledged." He describes it as the type of lingering loneliness we experience even while we enjoy meaningful relationships with God and others. He says it is inevitable and a result of the fall. Core loneliness is even necessary, Varney claims, because it makes us long for eternity, when God will wipe away every tear and welcome us into perfect fellowship.

Perhaps some who submit to the Loneliness Project have more going on beneath the surface. They are rightly grieved by the loss of a friend or loved one, a recent move, or parents who treat them poorly. But they may also be suffering from the effects of core loneliness, a loneliness untouched by improved circumstances. Great loneliness makes us yearn for the Great Belonging, even if we don't know how to put words around our affliction or our ache for more.

$$\left(\begin{array}{c} 3 \end{array}\right)$$

Wandering around the Stacks

Conversations about certain topics often prompt feelings of lonely difference: politics, religion, social justice, life priorities, and vocation. I am too conservative for some, too liberal for others. Maybe you are too religious for some, too secular for others. She is too focused on people on the margins for some, too selfish for others. He is too quirky for some, too ordinary for others. I am too literary for some, too colloquial for others. And so it goes.

The isolation we feel when we are different can lead to loneliness. Rationally we may realize that we are, in fact, not so different from other people in our lives. But during those times when it seems like I am too otherly, I can sink into a state of despair.

Imagine you are wandering between stacks and stacks of boxes filled with people who don't mind being put into boxes. You could climb into one and thus have a more defined and agreeable identity, but you choose to wander around and in between the stacks of boxes by yourself, peering in and chatting every so often with those inside. Those of us who avoid climbing in the boxes may always feel like we don't belong. At least we have each other. Maybe? When we are fortunate enough to bump into someone else who's wandering around the stacks, we have a good chance of meeting a kindred spirit. But our relationships with other box avoiders aren't quite like the relationships box dwellers have with each other. Our relationships are looser, more nuanced, more transient. We are a bit lonelier.

A couple of weeks ago my spiritual director, Susan, asked if I had thought about Jesus's loneliness. It would make sense for me to think about Jesus's loneliness—given that I'm a Christian writing a book about loneliness and all—but I hadn't. (One reason I love having a spiritual director is that she always asks great questions.) But when I did think about it, I was struck by how intense his loneliness must have been. According to the Gospels, Jesus had plenty of company—sometimes too much company—but I can imagine his differentness might have felt significant. He was God-man among very many not-God-men and not-God-women. He was the ultimate wanderer between the stacks, never choosing just one box for himself but visiting among them all. He was also abandoned and rejected, betrayed by one disciple, denied by another. And he endured a horrific death that no one else has ever known or will ever know. I can't truly compare my otherness to Jesus's otherness, but recognizing he was acquainted with an intense loneliness no one else will ever know does help.

Susan also encouraged me to ask what God is doing with my loneliness. What purpose does God have for me in my predicament? *Is* it a predicament? How might God use my suffering?

I often find conversing about loneliness—or conversing alongside loneliness—with other people has, ironically, invited me into places of intimacy. This seems especially true when I think about the conversations I have with my teenage daughter. Because I know some of what she experiences, I am able to empathize with her. Even though she hates feeling isolated and despises her core loneliness, God gave her a mom who can listen and understand where she is coming from when her loneliness flares up into engulfing flames. My listening helps the fire die down into a smoldering and smoky presence less crushing to her soul. Knowing our conversations are a gift to my daughter redeems some of my loneliness. It makes me feel more connected to her and sustains me in my isolation.

A 2018 survey examined the opinions on loneliness and relationships of more than fifty thousand adults. One of the most surprising findings was the stigma that people attach to loneliness—but only their own, not that of others. "People didn't think badly of other lonely individuals at all," a researcher for the study said. "But people who scored high on loneliness felt very negatively about themselves, and so they would conceal it—they felt there was a real shame in telling other people."

I feel some of that shame too, and shame is one reason loneliness can be so awful. While I have been aware of my loneliness for much of my life, I had rarely spoken of it to others until recently. I'd tried to ignore it, deny it, or distract myself from it through busyness, social media, TV shows, an extra glass of wine, work, writing, and looking to my husband, kids, and friends to provide more than they could provide. Emily White, author of *Lonely*, believes avoiding the topic of loneliness can make our loneliness worse: "The more you try to pretend it's not a problem, the more central and significant it might begin to seem."

Admitting I struggle with loneliness, talking about it, and writing about it have helped me let go of shame. When we perceive loneliness as a common condition instead of some sort of unique abnormality, we are less likely to be ashamed. When we participate in conversations about our loneliness, its triggers, and its balms, we have opportunities to offer empathy. And when this happens, some of the power it has over us is destroyed. Otherness dwindles, boxes collapse, belonging swells.

Here's to destroying the power of loneliness.

$$\bigl(\,4\,\bigr)$$

A Fragile Knowledge

My earliest memory of feeling alone is when I went to a week-long YMCA summer day camp. I was maybe four or five years old. I knew no one except my older brother, and back then he wanted nothing to do with me. I don't think I said more than a few words to anyone at camp for the full five days, and the aloneness was devastating.

Somewhere along the way, after I entered elementary school, I began to feel lonely even when I wasn't alone. At the time, I didn't know my first feelings of loneliness were tied to my awareness that everything was not okay. Everyone around me acted like everything was just fine and expected me to do the same: I'm fine. You're fine. We're all fine!

But I knew, even as a child, about tornadoes and missing children and drunk drivers. I knew about death, violence, sadness. I knew we all were capable of flinging unkind words toward each other. I knew we *weren't* fine. I held a glass globe filled with all of this fragile knowledge inside me, and I was afraid speaking up and naming our not-fineness would shatter the globe into hundreds of shards. It would only cause more harm.

So I remained in the solitude of my silence. I did my best to convince myself and everyone else I was just fine.

5

The Weight Pressing
Down on Us

My first therapist told me some of us feel loneliness more deeply than others and I am probably one of those people. When he spoke those words I knew I was made for therapy. I had been waiting my whole life to have someone explain myself to me. It was as if something lifted, like a helium-filled balloon escaping the fist of a young child. The only other time I had felt that sort of discernible relief from the weight pressing down on me was when I first understood the truth of the gospel—it wasn't up to me to get everything right or figure everything out. Jesus made me lighter, and my therapist did too.

I don't remember much about the appointment other than those words. It was fifteen years ago, when I was a young mother of a one-year-old baby girl. I've had dozens of other therapy appointments over the years. I'm sure I was sitting on a sofa.

There's always a sofa for sitting, except in the cartoons and the movies, where the sofa is for lying down. But I always sit. I toss the throw pillows aside and make myself comfortable, usually in one of the corners. I feel more stable in the corner than I do floating around in the middle without anything holding me up.

My former therapist is a kind man with kind eyes who cries with his clients when tears are an appropriate response. I used to think my tears were a sign of weakness—proof there was something wrong with me, and I definitely did not want to appear weak or flawed. This man taught me how to grieve and sorrow over things that are worthy of grief and sorrow.

I don't remember if I cried when he told me I felt loneliness more deeply than some people. But if I think about that moment long enough, it moves me to tears.

(6)

Occasions of Loneliness

1. You wake up in a strange place.
2. You wake up in a familiar place with a beloved one lying next to you.
3. You long for your childhood home.
4. You long for your grandmother's home.
5. You long for somewhere you've never been.
6. You're sick on your birthday.
7. No one remembers your birthday.
8. You're a new employee in a new office and you plan to eat lunch alone.
9. You're on the outside of the inside jokes.
10. You have a secret that you will never tell.
11. Your older sister leaves for college.
12. Your oldest child leaves for college.
13. Your best friend's wedding.

14. You visit a new church for the first time.
15. You visit a new church for the second time. And the third.
16. Hospital smells.
17. Hospital sounds.
18. The anniversary of your mother's death, your husband's death.
19. You remember that you forgot the anniversary of your mother's death.
20. You turn out the lights before going to sleep, when all you have left are yourself and your thoughts.

A Breakdown

Loneliness is not always tame.

In 2007 I had a full-blown psychotic breakdown, landing me in an inpatient psychiatric facility for eight days and revealing previously undiagnosed and untreated bipolar I disorder. Insanity, as they say in the world of psychoanalysis, is overdetermined. That is, it has more than one cause. Many desires and fears ignited my episode. It was an exhausting season for me as a stay-at-home mom. While I loved my children, I felt like I was trapped in a prison of the daily, ordinary tasks required to care for them and run a household. We had recently built and moved into a new home. And we were enmeshed in a church drama that created ripples in our faith community, rattled our beliefs, and filled us with questions and doubt. I might have been able to recover from any one of those stressors—the demands of the children, the move, the church. But all together, they were too much for my brain to process and manage. I cracked.

One of the worst symptoms of my mental illness was loneliness. To be more precise, loneliness was one of the most predictable and yet most surprising symptoms. I had always been familiar with loneliness, but I could not have foreseen how my sense of isolation would intensify when I first fell into mental illness. Dear friends pulled away, and acquaintances avoided me. And because my mind was jumbled and confused, I felt separated from myself.

I had long been formed by the language of the Psalms, and so somewhere in the sorrow of loneliness and my new diagnosis, I turned to them. In moments during which I had the ability to focus on Scripture, I'd meditate on a psalm or two or three. Over time I began to experience the power of the psalter in a new way. I discovered the Psalms were a cradle in which I could rest.

One passage I clung to during this season was Psalm 31:1-4.

> In you, O Lord, I seek refuge;
>> do not let me ever be put to shame;
>> in your righteousness deliver me.
> Incline your ear to me;
>> rescue me speedily.
> Be a rock of refuge for me,
>> a strong fortress to save me.
> You are indeed my rock and my fortress;
>> for your name's sake lead me and guide me,
> take me out of the net that is hidden for me,
>> for you are my refuge.

In my depression, I read and reread the psalmist's words. Although David and I were many generations and circumstances apart, I tried to make his declarations and longings for God my own. And while David's words were mine for the taking, they weren't magical. They gave me a framework to speak to God and helped me know God was near, but I was still sick. I was still lonely.

A story in 1 Samuel 16 describes a scene in which Saul was being tormented by "an evil spirit." To comfort Saul, his servants sought a skillful musician to play for him. One man told Saul about a lyre player he knew—a son of Jesse. So Saul sent messengers to Jesse and requested the presence of his son. The story continues:

> David came to Saul, and entered his service. Saul loved him greatly, and he became his armor-bearer. And Saul sent to Jesse, saying, "Let David remain in my service, for he has found favor in my sight." And whenever the evil spirit from God came upon Saul, David took the lyre and played it with his hand, and Saul would be relieved and feel better, and the evil spirit would depart from him. (1 Sam 16:21-23)

Some commentators have concluded from these verses that Saul suffered from depression. Some say David played and sang psalms for Saul and the familiar words soothed his desolation. Since the Psalms are often described as the language of our souls, it's possible Saul was comforted by both the encouraging psalms of gratitude and the desperate psalms of lament.

During a season of deep depression following my manic episode, I started praying the Liturgy of the Hours. The Liturgy of the Hours, also known as the Divine Office, is a set of daily prayers that incorporates psalms, hymns, and readings. One description explains that the hymns and litanies "integrate the prayer of the Psalms into the age of the Church, expressing the symbolism of the time of day, the liturgical season, or the feast being celebrated." Sometimes I used a prayerbook, and other times I prayed in the company of online recordings. When I listened online, ringing church bells invited me into prayer, followed by the call, "God, come to my assistance," and the response, "Lord, make haste to help me."

The prayers and psalms unified my heart and mind and provided language for the sundry songs of my soul. I listened to morning prayers on the days when I had a few minutes to myself. I listened to evening prayers most nights when my husband and I were in bed, after we'd turned out the lights.

The rhythm of the opening hymn, followed by the recitation of the Psalms and prayers, helped me connect to my past, present, and future selves. The prayers also joined me to others around the world who were praying the exact same words. This awareness of global, communal prayers allowed me to see my loneliness, depression, and difficult circumstances more clearly. Yes, I was suffering. But I was also a part of the church at prayer, and I knew somehow my sorrows were being divided. I knew the joy of others was in part my joy, too. When I was listening to and meditating on psalms of praise, I held onto those words because I had proclaimed them in the past and I knew I would be able to proclaim them again in the future. I also held onto those words because others in the church could boldly proclaim them even if my own attempts felt dishonest. Listening to the recitation and chanting of the Psalms, prayers, and hymns reminded me my faith isn't just my own. My faith also belongs to the faith of others. When my faith falters, the faith of others fills the lull.

Time, therapy, and the right combinations of medications helped make me well. Six months after that late-night trip to the emergency room, I experienced the beginnings of a re-belonging to myself, and I became a more recognizable version of the person others knew. My brain was working more like it had before my illness. I was able to care for my children as a healthier mother, relate to my husband as a partner instead of a patient, and reestablish some of my friendships.

A portion of my loneliness endured, yes. But through my engagement with the Psalms and liturgical prayers, God bridled the wildness of the isolation stalking me. What was once untamed God caught, soothed, softened.

$$\left(\;8\;\right)$$

Befriended by the Ordinary

There were years of calm, and then a second bout of mania. And then in 2011, after days of hiding in my bedroom and trying to adjust to even higher doses of psychiatric medications, even though I was still experiencing some mania, it was time for me to reenter more of my ordinary life. My psychiatrist and therapist told me to incorporate some day-to-day activities despite the mania and paranoia. It was difficult and overwhelming, but I tried to do what they recommended. I knew I couldn't stay alone in my bed forever, scrolling through Twitter and eating M&Ms. Here is the story of a day from the middle of that year.

Tim wakes me and places a cup of coffee on the desk next to my side of the bed. He began bringing coffee to me in bed during my first manic episode, and he has continued to do so almost every morning since. I recently read a sobering statistic stating that more than 90 percent of marriages with one person diagnosed with bipolar disorder will end in divorce. I don't know what the rate of divorce is for marriages with one person diagnosed with bipolar disorder and one person who brings her coffee in bed every morning. Surely it's less than 90 percent.

I wrap both hands around the warm ceramic mug and drink, thinking through what lies before me. I need to get out of bed, get dressed, brush my teeth, walk my dog, care for my children, prepare meals, and interact with my husband and others who might cross my path. I wonder how I'm going to make it and am tempted to give up before I begin. But I want to be well. Staying in bed, isolating myself, and tuning out is a mirage in a desert. It seems to offer me what I need, but it will not give me the life I want. I tell myself to plant my feet on the floor and stand up. I am in motion. I move forward and fight against what makes more sense.

I proceed through the day and adjust my focus to what's right before me instead of the whole picture. While I'm with my children, managing their exposure to screens and refereeing their arguments, I'm on autopilot. I remember the consuming guilt during my first manic episode when I couldn't care for them well. This time I know they are okay. They are safe and content. They have my presence, even though I'm not fully present. We're making it, and that's enough for now.

I gather and sort the piles of laundry. I throw a load of white towels into the washing machine. Twenty minutes later, I move them to the dryer. After an hour, they are clean and dry. I fold the warm towels and put them away in the bathroom cabinet, and I suddenly realize there is not much room for paranoia in the midst of these daily, mindless tasks. My body and mind have moved through these motions so many times, so I know the choreography by heart. What I used to experience as drudgery is now a comfortable, familiar dance with a safe friend.

I make a pot of chicken, white bean, and rosemary soup. It's the same recipe I used before I was diagnosed. It is the recipe I will use in twenty years. It's the recipe I use if I am manic or depressed or somewhere in-between. Soaking beans, sautéing onions, chopping chicken, and breathing in the aroma of the rosemary connects me to a healthier version of myself in the midst of my sickness.

My daughter wanders into the kitchen while the soup is simmering. She inhales deeply and says, "I wish you were the type of mom who baked cupcakes." I laugh and notice it's the first time I've laughed in weeks. "It would be nice to smell chocolate cupcakes instead of your white bean soup," she adds. I pull her into a hug and make a promise, "I'll make chocolate cupcakes soon. Will you help?"

My dog and I meander through the neighborhood along our usual route. With each step along the familiar path, truth reveals itself more and more to my tortured mind, like the late June sun leaving its mark on my face. The blooming orange daylilies and pink and blue hydrangeas in my neighbors' yards serve as beacons. They help me remember the past and hope for the future. I begin to believe I'll come out on the other side, I'll be able to return to myself.

And I do. Six weeks later I wake with the morning, and the mania and paranoia are gone. It's as if someone stood up and said, "We're all done here. You can return to yourself, your family, your community." Sometimes the mundane seems changed by the memory of the mania. But mostly I feel accompanied, befriended by all this ordinariness.

$$\bigcirc 9$$

Our Pets Who Bring Us Joy

The Episcopal Church of Saint Francis Assisi in Birmingham, Alabama, is one of the many churches committed to celebrating the Feast of St. Francis. Every October churches across the country honor Francis of Assisi, who was said to have a special kinship with animals, by inviting people to bring their pets to church and blessing them.

Before the service began, the nave filled with people and their pets—dogs of various breeds and dispositions. Small reptiles. A rabbit. A hedgehog. While we settled into our seats, a bluegrass trio from a local Presbyterian church crooned "Just a Little Talk with Jesus." During the sermon, enhanced by plenty of yelps and barks and pants, the Reverend Jamie McAdams made sure those in attendance knew a fuller story of St. Francis, which extends beyond his love for all creatures great and small.

He explained while St. Francis is the patron saint of our dear pets, he was primarily a man of faith. Born into a wealthy family, he became a Christian at a young age, gave everything he had to the poor, and lived a life of solitude and worship, eventually founding the Franciscan order and movement. "We are not talking about a person who wields superhuman powers," Reverend McAdams said. "He was meek. He was mild. He had such an affinity for the creation of God that he was in tune with all of it, including the creatures, the trees, and everything else."

Reverend McAdams tied the life of St. Francis to the day's Gospel reading, which came from Matthew 11:25-30. The last few verses of that passage contain relatively well-known words of Jesus: "Come to me, all you that are weary and are carrying heavy burdens, and I will give you rest. Take my yoke upon you and learn from me; for I am gentle and humble in heart, and you will find rest for your souls. For my yoke is easy, and my burden is light" (Matt 11:28-30). Reverend McAdams said one way those who are weary and burdened can have peace and rest is through interacting with a pet. He shared several studies showing people who have a dog or a cat or a guinea pig have a better quality of life. They also live longer, are more prepared to fight off depression, and are less likely to struggle with loneliness. He continued his sermon, pointing out that while people may find comfort in all sorts of things, ultimate peace can only be found in Jesus. Reverend McAdams preached the good news—he reminded us Jesus is the only one who can fully satisfy our desire when we are tired and weary.

Following the sermon and the passing of the peace, while the bluegrass musicians sang Johnny Cash's "Redemption" and the hymn "What a Friend We Have in Jesus," all pets and their owners were invited up front to form a circle. Reverend McAdams and another member of the clergy walked around the circle and blessed each dog, rabbit, hedgehog, and lizard. As everyone returned to their pews, Reverend McAdams went outside to perform his final blessings for the two horses visible to the congregation through a wall full of large windows. The horses were sturdy and stately animals with chestnut-colored coats. They stood with an attentive calmness and seemed pleased to receive his attention while he stroked their sides and spoke blessings over them.

Several studies have indeed shown the many psychological benefits of pet ownership. In a 2019 study, 80 percent of pet owners said their pets help them combat their loneliness. The study's researchers concluded, "When it comes to both pet owners and non–pet owners, 85 percent of respondents believe interaction with a companion animal can help reduce loneliness and 76 percent agree human-animal interactions can help address social isolation. Further, pet owners with the closest bond to their pet see the highest positive impact on their feelings of loneliness and social isolation." And *Time* magazine reported on a recent poll by the University of Michigan, which found almost 90 percent of older pet owners believed animals improved their lives and made them feel loved.

Several years ago, I went to a local lunchtime meetup of people working in media and communications. Halfway through our meal, I found myself listening to a conversation about two older dogs living in the boarding area at a nearby veterinarian's office. The dogs' original owner had mental and physical disabilities and had been dead for seven years. Before she died, however, her caregivers had promised they would never separate the dogs, whom she had named Puppy and Happy. A home for both of them had never been found.

When I heard about these two elderly dogs, who were believed to be fourteen years old, and how they were sharing a cage in a boarding area and exposed to the natural elements because they had never been adopted, I had to do something. Later that day, after I picked my kids up from school, we drove to the vet's office and asked if we could take Puppy and Happy for a walk. Bearing no resemblance whatsoever, they were both mutts who had found their way to their owner over the span of a year or so. Puppy had a dark charcoal gray fluffy coat, while Happy was a beagle mix with light brown and white markings. Puppy and Happy weren't blood sisters, but they were practically joined at the hip. A few days later, I brought them home for a two-week "trial period," which made Tim laugh. "There's no way you're taking those dogs back," he told me that night.

Tim was right. I never returned the dogs. I became their primary caregiver, walking them at least three times each day, feeding them a mixture of expensive wet and dry dog food formulated specially for older dogs, and providing cozy, plush beds for their geriatric joints. Because they were so old, they were largely inactive. They enjoyed our leisurely walks and liked to ride in my car while I ran errands. They followed me around the house as I did laundry, prepared meals, and cared for my children. They became my shadows, and my fondness for them grew deep and wide. I once jokingly told friends our home had become a palliative care center for older dogs.

Indeed, just a few weeks later, Puppy died from complications during a surgical procedure related to her recent cancer diagnosis.

We had only known Puppy for a few months when she died. As I left the house to take her to the vet for her surgery, Happy watched us walk out the back door. Then she turned, looked at my husband, squatted, and peed in the middle of our living room rug. It was likely the first time in more than a dozen years that the two dogs had been separated.

After I returned home without her sister, Happy refused to eat and lost much of her vigor. Two days after Puppy died, to coax her into eating, I gave her a large portion of a hot, fresh rotisserie chicken. She gobbled it up and later ate a bowl of her dog food. Every time I brought a rotisserie chicken home after buying groceries, Happy would follow me in the kitchen, stand by my side, and stare at me with her pleading, oh-so-sad eyes until I deboned some for her.

Happy became more attached to me after Puppy was gone, and I welcomed her loyalty and presence. Two years after we first adopted Puppy and Happy, I had my second major manic episode and subsequent period of significant depression. During my first intense bout of mania and depression four years earlier, my loneliness had been excruciating. But this time around, I had Happy. She stayed by my side day and night. While I was sick, I let her onto our bed while I rested and waited for my meds to kick in and stabilize my brain. She would jump up onto the bed, settle herself down, stretch out beside one of my legs, and prop her head on my ankle.

Her companionship made my illness less isolating. She probably sensed something was off, but she still expected me to take her for walks, feed her, and care for her. That was my job. That was what I did. While Tim and my parents and various babysitters relieved me of most of my childcare duties, Happy wouldn't let me pass her off to anyone else. And my recovery was quicker because of her. As we walked along our usual routes throughout our neighborhood, and as I performed my regular duties for her, I slowly remembered who I was. She was my mental health doula. Happy helped me return to who I was before I got sick. She helped me belong to myself anew.

When Happy died three years later at the age of nineteen, I was devastated. Even though no one was shocked by her death, I grieved for days, remembering the joy and cheer she provided. I even wrote a terrible poem about our shared time and the ebb and flow of life together.

When I think of the many pets and their owners from the St. Francis Day service and remember the love I had for Puppy and Happy, I am filled with gratitude for the faithful animal friends God has given us. They are evidence of God's goodness to all of us whose loneliness is lightened by our pets and the comfort and warmth they provide.

An Illustration

An illustration by my friend and Birmingham artist Jamison Harper hangs on a wall in my living room, above a pair of turquoise velvet swivel chairs, near the entrance to our small kitchen. Jamie's digital drawing accompanies an essay I wrote for a church magazine, about the gifts of the Psalms in my illness and in my health.

This work depicts a lone, wild-haired woman surrounded by various shades of pink and purple. One side of her face is at peace and resting; an eye cast downward in contemplation, a hand held up in a gesture of prayer or praise. The other side of her face is crazed, with a wide-eyed expression of despair and a pained hand begging God—or anyone—for relief. I imagine she feels isolated and othered in her divided self. She is pulled in two directions, while forces beyond her control play tug-of-war with her mind and soul.

Jamie's art captures the essence of the Psalms, displaying the two farthest points of the psalter's spectrum. It also captures the essence of me—one who knows the loneliness of pain, the belonging of peace, and the expanse between the two. But I don't love this illustration because it's a portrait of me. I love it because it displays the paradox of humanity: replete with both vigor and infirmity, both fracture and repair.

$$\left(11 \right)$$

When Your Mother's Soul Has Left You

Germans have a word for intense loneliness, for a feeling of utter abandonment: *mutterseelenallein*. Translated, it means "your mother's soul has left you," and it's used in the context of being so alone that no soul—not even your mother's—is near. That's a heartbreaking level of loneliness. A German broadcasting company that promotes understanding between different cultures says:

Even though the word sounds like a typical German word—or rather three German words pasted together into one long German adjective—the term actually derived from the French idiom "moi tout seul," meaning "me all alone." When the Huguenots, a group of persecuted French Protestants, fled to Germany in the 18th century, they used the term "moi tout seul" to describe their feeling of isolation and dislocation from home. But the Germans misunderstood the phrase as "mutterseelen" (mother's souls) and added the word "allein" (alone) so that the phrase would make sense to them.

I came across a version of the word, *mutterseelig*, in an early version of "Snow White" from one of the earliest Grimm fairy tale manuscripts written in 1810. Oliver Loo, who translated this manuscript into English with several fascinating annotations, decided to keep some words in German to "eliminate the possibility of trying to find just the right English word for a story and picking one that is close but does not convey the full meaning of the original word." So he chose to keep *mutterseelig* and explained what it means. He wrote, "*mutterseelig* alone" is "mother + soul from *moi teut seul* in French meaning 'I all alone.' Completely alone."

This word appears only once in the entire manuscript, when Snow White is in the forest and about to be killed by the hunter who has been ordered by the jealous queen to kill her beautiful daughter. (In this version of the fairy tale, the queen is Snow White's biological mother, not her stepmother.) After Snow White escapes the hands of her potential murderer, she is in the large forest, frightened and "*mutterseelig* alone." Not only is Snow White alone—by herself and without anyone to protect her—but she has been abandoned by her mother and her mother's soul.

Why is the deepest loneliness one can feel the sort that occurs when the mother's soul has left?

Roland Barthes was a French literary theorist, philosopher, and critic who lived most of his life with his mother. After she died in 1977, Barthes began a diary of mourning. His thoughts were recorded on many small slips of paper and later gathered and published as *Mourning Diary*. An entry dated October 27 reads, "Everyone guesses—I feel this—the degree of a bereavement's intensity. But it's impossible (meaningless, contradictory signs) to measure how much someone is afflicted." In another entry he writes, "Solitude = having no one at home to whom you can say: I'll be back at a specific time or who you can call to say (or to whom you can just say): *voilà,* I'm home now." Words from November 21 recall a specific sort of grief: "Since *maman's* death, a sort of digestive weakness—as if I were suffering precisely where she took the greatest care of me: food."

And an especially heartsick entry from December 23, 1978, more than a year after his mother's death, puts into words what many may feel after their mothers die:

> Little disappointments, attacks, threats, worries, sense of failure, dark times, heavy burden to carry, "penal servitude," etc. I can't help putting all that in relation to *maman's* death. It's not that (simple magic) she's no longer here to protect me . . . but rather—or is it the same thing? that now I'm reduced to *initiating myself to the world*—a harsh initiation. Miseries of a birth.

I'm struck by the tragic idea that those whose mothers have died have to be born anew in order to learn how to re-navigate the world because the women who birthed them are gone.

In *Mourning Diary*, we see Barthes exploring new emotional and physical landscapes his mother's death has formed. We listen to his feelings of sadness mixed with the guilt that comes when hope glimmers. He also coins a term to name his new reality: "abandonitis." It's this sense of abandonment that *mutterseelenallein* evokes.

Every now and then, the reality of death pursues me the way a lion stalks its prey. When this happens, I worry about how I will die, when I will die, and whom I will leave behind. My most significant worry about death relates to imagining how it will affect my kids. I truly believe if I were to die today or tomorrow or next week, my children would ultimately be okay. They would grieve. They would be afflicted in a multitude of ways. They would feel abandoned.

But one day—hopefully sooner rather than later—they would thrive again. Hopefully, they would create new and deeper intimacies with others, and their sense of abandonment would be eased.

$$\left(12 \right)$$

Linger and Listen

A few months ago I listened to a recorded talk a visiting theo-logian and author had given to the clergy and staff at my church. He said many things I agree with about what it means to be a Christian who is loved by a good and gracious God. But when someone asked him a question about loneliness, he said many things that baffled and saddened me. He rambled on for several minutes about the nature of loneliness with a tone and demeanor of authority. But his approach was to simplify loneliness, call it a result of mental illness, and tell his audience how to fix it.

When I finished listening to his talk, I felt like an outcast. I'm a Christian who lives with a mental illness and sometimes struggles with loneliness even when I'm healthy. I felt indicted for not having enough faith or friends. My mind spiraled down into a dark place, where I wondered if I even belonged with other Christians. I asked myself why I was hitching myself to people who were so different from me. Why did I want to associate with those who were so terrified of the nuances and paradoxes of loneliness?

Lauren Winner writes about the idea of staying with loneliness in her book *Still*:

> I used to say to Ruth, in all those tortured months before I left my husband, that what I feared most was loneliness. Not being alone, which I find perfect and peaceful, but loneliness, which makes me want to die, which makes me think I *will* die, which I will do anything to avoid feeling: call a friend; go shopping; pedal endless, frantic miles on my stationary bike; pour another drink; take another sleeping pill.
>
> What Ruth says is: Maybe I should try to stay in that loneliness, just for five minutes, just for ten minutes. Maybe the loneliness has something for me. Maybe I should see what that something is.

I love Ruth's advice about loneliness, and I think it can be applied to many uncomfortable emotions. We are so quick to try to escape our discomfort and difficulties instead of receiving them and responding to them with a desire to learn. Sometimes we can look back on the hard things we've experienced and recognize how we've grown after the fact. But what would happen if we had a curious posture in the *midst* of the hard things? What if, instead of telling his audience how to fix loneliness, that speaker had invited them to sit with loneliness and listen to it?

I'm not saying we call a thing what it isn't. We still call the hard things hard. But instead of running away or numbing ourselves, we can choose to stay. We can give our attention to the present moment, and we can ask our feelings what they might have for us.

After listening to this speaker, I decided not to take his advice. Rather than approaching my loneliness as something to be fixed, I decided to approach it as a companion to whom to listen. Sitting with the heaviness of differentness for half an hour or so revealed a deep fear of rejection. Underneath my loneliness, I was afraid those who listened to this man talk—the leaders of my church—would agree with him: loneliness represents a fundamental flaw; it is a symptom of poor mental health; anyone who struggles with it is deficient in some way. I was worried they would reject me for struggling with and exploring loneliness. Loneliness wasn't my problem. Fear was. So I acknowledged the thick blanket of fright covering me and threw it aside. When I let go of the fear, the pang of isolation subsided too.

My loneliness will return. And my fear of rejection may return too. But being curious about my emotions taught me something I needed to know about myself. Loneliness doesn't always teach me a nice lesson. Sometimes it offers me a chance to slow down and encourages me to reach out to my husband or a friend. Sometimes it asks me to grieve the loss of a relationship or the loss of what I hoped a relationship might one day become. At other times my loneliness is silent, with nothing to give—a child with her jaw clenched tight and her arms crossed, stubborn and refusing to speak. But I want to keep sitting with her whenever she shows up, because I never know when she might open her arms and pull me close. I never know when she might whisper some wisdom into my ear.

13

Hot and Cold

In a 2008 study, Chen-Bo Zhang and Geoffrey J. Leonardelli explored connections between temperature and feelings of loneliness. They wrote, "Loneliness and coldness seem to go side by side in everyday language" and shared how the 1970s song "Lonely This Christmas" illustrates this occurence. The song's lyrics tell the story of someone who will be alone and cold because of the emptiness forged by the absence of a former lover.

But are temperature and loneliness linked on any registers beyond the metaphorical? Or as the subtitle of Zhong and Leonardelli's article says, "Does Social Exclusion Literally Feel Cold?" They concluded it's possible we use words like *frigid*, *icy*, and *cold* to describe social interactions because we notice how "the experience of coldness and the experience of social rejection collide." Their experiments found people actually felt colder or preferred to eat something warm when they felt lonely. These findings are in line with theories of embodied cognition, which suggest our social experiences are not always separate from our bodily experiences. In other words, we feel in our bodies what we experience in our relationships. It's as if our bodies are thermometers, registering in bone and skin and muscle the temperature of our lives and the condition of our inclusion.

Zhang and Leonardelli's findings may also explain why I enjoy a roaring fire in my living room fireplace with a hot toddy on a dreary winter night, why I own so many soup cookbooks, and why I love removing clean towels from the dryer as soon as the buzzer sounds. These moments of warmth provide doses of belonging, ease my core loneliness, and make me forget, for a bit, that I will never be fully known.

Our Five Senses

It's tempting to think of belonging and loneliness as primarily emotional experiences, but we are whole beings who inhabit this world in our physical bodies. We hold loneliness in tense necks and crossed arms. We hold belonging in confident postures and friendly smiles.

We might think of the embodiment of loneliness only when considering its pathologies. Medical studies show chronic feelings of isolation can have a negative effect on one's physical health. Loneliness can contribute to heart disease, type 2 diabetes, arthritis, and more. Lonely people are also twice as likely to develop Alzheimer's disease. Isolation increases the production of stress hormones, harms sleep, and impairs cognitive abilities. These effects of loneliness produce chronic inflammation, which lowers immunity to the degree that lonely people can experience worse symptoms from the common cold. The chronic stress of loneliness can also age the body more quickly and cause extensive damage to one's overall well-being.

But if our bodies can register the trauma of loneliness, they can also console us during loneliness and help find its antidotes. Specifically, our senses can console. Our bodies' abilities to see, smell, hear, taste, and touch assist us as we process our emotions so our minds don't have to do all of the work. The five senses help us notice and respond to the world around us. They form a bridge between the external and the internal, providing connection points that enable us to remember who we were, recognize who we are, and dream about who we want to become. Our senses help us belong to our various selves held together by the past, present, and future.

With our sense of smell, we take in aromas that remind us of certain seasons or specific moments when we felt safe and sure of who we were. When it rains, the smell reminds me of the freedom of my childhood and how I would return outside after a summer shower to play in the park across the street from my house or search for tadpoles in a nearby stream. Decades later, when I sit on my balcony on a drizzly afternoon, the scent of rain settles and soothes me.

With our sense of hearing, we listen to songs that rekindle feelings from years ago or a week ago, when we felt more secure in our identities. I hear a song by the band R.E.M. and think of high school and the hours and hours I spent by myself in my bedroom, singing along happily or choreographing silly dances to show my friends the next time we were together.

With our sense of taste, we savor food that makes us more aware of our desires and cravings. I grab a bowl out of my kitchen cabinet and add a cup or so of plain Greek yogurt. I sprinkle it with sea salt and za'atar and drizzle it with extra virgin olive oil. Every nourishing bite of this meal, which I make often when I don't have to worry about what anyone else wants or needs, brings me home to myself.

Sometimes I think of loneliness as a sort of mindfulness bell calling me to query my senses. If I am feeling lonely in a particular moment, I ask myself, What am I seeing, tasting, touching, hearing, and smelling? Are there any connections between my senses and this particular feeling of loneliness? How can I engage my senses so I can have a more significant connection to myself and this present moment?

An example: my children's experience of drinking hot chocolate. It doesn't snow much where we live, maybe once every year or two. But whenever it snows, I make homemade hot chocolate for them to drink after they're done playing outside. They strip off their soaked coats, hats, and gloves, and sit down at the kitchen table. Still exhilarated from the novelty of their snow adventures, they sip hot chocolate while we discuss who got hit with snowballs and how fun it was to slide down the hill by our house.

Feelings of joy and connection might be associated with the sight, aroma, and taste of hot chocolate for the rest of their lives. When they are adults and feeling lonely or blue, I hope they pull out the cocoa powder, milk, sugar, and vanilla extract and make a serving or two of hot chocolate. As they sip the warm, sweet beverage and recall happy snow-filled memories, I hope they remember who they were and marvel at who they've become. I hope a comfortable belonging enfolds them, protects them from the stings of isolation, and heals their wounds of desolation.

Part II

BELONGING
TO EACH OTHER

Potential

Coworking spaces reveal something interesting about loneliness and connection. Many people pay to work in a communal space instead of working from home or renting an office so they can have access to a network of other freelancers and entrepreneurs. According to a survey by researchers at the University of Michigan's Ross School of Business, people who work at coworking spaces report a level of thriving that approaches a six on a seven-point scale. The results suggest several reasons coworkers thrive at such a high level; one is that people who work in coworking spaces feel like they are part of a community.

That all makes sense, doesn't it? But here's the surprising finding from the research: even those who interact less often with others from their coworking space still felt a strong sense of identity with their coworking community. Coworking space managers often host events and other networking opportunities for their members. Some coworking spaces have "lunch and learns" and happy hour gatherings to encourage members to be on friendly terms with each other. None of the social functions are required, of course, and some people choose to not participate. But it didn't matter. The survey results suggested the *potential* for interactions helps form feelings of connection with other coworkers—even when members don't regularly take advantage of them. Coworking spaces appear to make people feel less lonely even if they rarely mingle with fellow coworkers.

Does this carry over into other realms? If a high school offers clubs of all shapes and sizes and purposes, do the students who never participate feel a sense of connection to other students because they know clubs are available to join? If a church offers Bible studies, small groups, potluck meals, do those who never show up feel connected to other members of their congregation? Does even the potential for connection give us hope?

$$\left(16\right)$$

When We Didn't Have Sex

When my husband and I returned home after our honeymoon at a lovely all-inclusive resort in Mexico, we stopped having sex every day. I'm sure this is normal. I assume most couples—even those who are happily and newly married—don't have sex every day. But I still remember the first night it didn't happen.

I remember lying awake in our tiny apartment, surrounded by the darkness. My new husband was sleeping, and I could hear the hum of our window air-conditioning unit. The reality began to set in. Our marriage wouldn't always be as intimate as it was when our days consisted of hours on the beach listening to the Counting Crows and drinking free, unlimited, watered-down adult beverages. We clung to our new marriage and union during that week in Cancun.

Then when we got back, we had to think about other things like going to work, paying bills, keeping our apartment somewhat clean, and preparing dinner every night. So I laid in the bed next to my sleeping husband when we didn't have sex, and I realized for the first time that my marriage wouldn't save me from my loneliness.

Together but Separate

I don't remember which came first, falling in love with Tim or wanting to be married to him. I like to think I fell in love with him first, and that my desire to be with him for the rest of my life was a natural response to that love. But maybe I wanted to be married, because that's what the women in my family did. I was the first woman in a line of at least four generations to not be married by the age of ninteteen, and I finally became a Mrs. at the ripe age of twenty-three. Sometimes when I reflect on how desperate I was to be married in those days, I thank God for putting Tim in the right place at the right time. I shudder to think about who I could have ended up with. Twenty-three-year-old me definitely had it in her to fall for someone who forty-four-year-old me couldn't imagine being married to. God knew who I needed— a kind, emotionally available, spiritually aware man who makes me laugh and helps me be a better version of myself. He's also a great kisser and tall enough to reach the highest shelves in our kitchen cabinets. I know it sounds corny to say my spouse is my best friend. But I have to say it: Tim is my best friend. He makes my loneliness less lonely.

When Tim and I started dating, we had many late-night talks on the phone or at my apartment or the house he shared with several of his friends. We told each other the stories of our lives. We discussed our hopes for the future. We wanted to know everything. My ballet. His basketball. My family. His family. My Montgomery. His New Orleans. My doubts. His doubts. Favorite music, food preferences, dream jobs.

I was a new Christian who was beginning to understand the truths of the gospel and grasp—or be grasped by—God's grace. My spiritual enthusiasm inspired Tim and helped him remember his conversion to Christianity five years before. We discussed deep things of life and faith from the beginning of our relationship, which instilled a sort of intimacy I had never shared with another man.

One night, soon after Tim and I started dating, my roommate at the time said to me, "Y'all are going to get married. Mark my word." I hoped she was right. Every cell of my being wanted her to be right. I felt wholly myself when I was with him. I didn't feel judged. I didn't have to pretend to be more spiritual or smarter or more interesting.

Twenty-three or so years after meeting Tim, I have to say our shared suffering is one of the main reasons I want to be married to him now. Our suffering has had many faces—job woes, unemployment, infertility, a colicky newborn, small children, church drama, dashed hopes, my mental illness, teenagers, and more. During our seasons of suffering, we have sought God and received comfort and hope. But we have also turned to each other for support the way heliotropic flowers turn toward the sun.

Another reason I want to be married to him now is he's unwilling to buy into the standard middle-class narrative others expect us to embrace. Two years ago we moved into a small condo, which many friends and acquaintances thought was a strange choice. Why, with two growing kids, would we choose to downsize to a home with one-third the living space of our former house?

We also approach parenting differently than many of our peers. We don't force our kids to be involved with our church's youth group. We don't ship them off every summer to pricey summer camps. We prefer to not know the ins and outs of our kids' school assignments, test grades, and project due dates. We try to let them experience failure without stepping in to save them.

But in the midst of what sometimes feels like being on the periphery of the mostly white, mostly Christian, and mostly suburban culture we inhabit in this season of life, I have Tim and he has me. While many around us are speaking a language we aren't interested in learning, we share a sort of secret code. In not being known or understood by most people around us, we are more known and understood by each other.

Even so, I sometimes feel lonely in my marriage. My feelings of marital loneliness come in small moments, such as when Tim doesn't understand why I rarely want to watch a movie, or why I am not more frugal with our finances, or why I need to possess so many books, or why I'm often jealous of his hotel stays when he travels for work.

But the loneliness comes more abidingly as well, and often in the area of vocation. As a writer and spiritual director, many of my days are filled with reading, writing, and giving attention to the spiritual dimensions of life. As a sales executive for a technology company, Tim has days filled with client calls, meetings, and multiple hours designing and pitching solutions that will help his customers' businesses flourish. Because of the nature of our work and what seems to be a lack of common tasks, responsibilities, and desires, sometimes it seems like we are two people wandering around the same uninhabited island on paths that never cross.

While I may want to read Tim a magnificent sentence from a novel, talk to him about the latest draft of an essay I'm working on, or share a spiritual aha moment, I'm hesitant to do so, because I know he's full of ruminations from his own workday, which are quite different from mine. Does he want to divert his thoughts away from the familiar and toward the lesser known? He may want to tell me about a conversation with a coworker, share his new idea for a technology solution, or update me on a specific way God ministered to him, but he's hesitant to do so because he thinks I'd rather consider how to revise an essay, toss around ideas for new pitches, or wonder how in the world I'm supposed to grow my platform.

Maybe there are ways to decrease the loneliness we feel. Maybe we need to resist the urge to pull back and avoid conversations we think the other isn't interested in having. Maybe we need to be more willing to invite each other into the mundane minutiae of our work and let go of the expectations we have about how the other should respond.

Some loneliness in marriage is likely inevitable. I recently read something by poet Julius Lester that gave me pause. He wrote, "If you live with a writer, you have to accept that there's a part of that person that simply does not belong to you. And it isn't personal. In another context, I'd say that's the part that belongs to God." Maybe Lester is right. Maybe some of my vocational loneliness with Tim is a consequence of me being a writer who has things rattling around in my soul and mind that are only for God.

Still, I'm inclined to think if Tim and I were both writers or both in academia or both in technology, we would have a greater sense of togetherness. I asked others about how this plays out in their marriages and their responses were mixed. One woman, a professor, told me, "My husband and I are both in the same department, and we still experience a significant amount of loneliness." A second interlocutor echoed this experience of being lonely even though she and her husband worked together. She said:

When my husband and I moved overseas for ministry work, we were in language school together and in the same office. We shared a lot of things, and at the end of the day there was nothing left to talk about. I used to look forward to talking about my day and hearing about his. This was gone. Also, we experienced a lot of the same stresses and disappointments and also struggled when one of us was fulfilled in work and the other wasn't or when one of us was excelling in language school and the other struggling. It created greater gaps between us. I don't know if we are the exception to the rule, but it proves to be a very hard season on our marriage. Now that we are back in the States, I am looking forward to the day when my husband is working out of the home again and we will get to reconnect at the end of each day and discuss our passions together, instead of sitting in the same room and feeling miles apart.

Quotidian loneliness in a mostly good marriage may be unavoidable. I was once talking about my sense of marital loneliness with a divorced friend, and in mid-sentence—mid-bite of pasta, I think—I froze. Maybe I sounded like a poor little rich girl. Maybe I should shut up and count my blessings. But my friend nodded and seemed to agree. She didn't tell me I had no right to mention my loneliness. Although I imagine the loneliness she sometimes feels as someone who is now unmarried differs from what I feel in my marriage, she has known the loneliness of marriage. She knows how the distinct quality of ordinary marital loneliness reveals unmet desired and empty spaces. Maybe it's impossible to escape unfulfilled desires and desolate spaces in all our relationships, even our relationships with ourselves.

Perhaps wedded loneliness is a gift—even for those in happy marriages—showing us no human intimacy will truly repair our feelings of isolation and disconnection. Loneliness, at its heart, is a longing for more closeness with God.

(18)

When We Do Have Sex

A friend recently asked me about sex and loneliness. She wanted to know why it was possible to feel connected and isolated at the same time, or in such rapid succession that the connection and isolation seem to happen in the same instant while having sex. I knew what she meant as soon as she asked her question. I have sometimes felt disconnected from Tim during sex or immediately following. It can seem like there's a transparent wall between us—an unseen but present barrier, even while I am also enjoying our bodies and our sexual connection.

Maybe this is why people have so often spoken of the feeling after orgasm as *la petite mort*, or "the little death." In an instant, there is closeness and intensity, and then there is a rapid fall from closeness and intensity. It's as if, in the intensity born of closeness, you fall exactly into yourself.

While thinking about my friend's question, I came across an online video of the Netherlands Dance Theatre's performance of a piece called *Petite Mort*, which was choreographed by the Czecho-slovakian dancer Jiří Kylián. Art often helps me understand when words fail to explain, so I pressed play and hoped for the best. In this gorgeous seventeen-minute dance, six couples move in ways that evoke arousal, intimacy, and separation. At one point, the men and women end up on the floor and roll away from each other. The women roll stage right and disappear into the wings. The men roll stage left and disappear into the wings. But this isn't the end of the dance. There is a pause, and then the dance continues. The dancers dance alone, move in and out of their coupling, and life goes on.

And of course, that is exactly what happens after sex, even if you fall asleep with your husband in your arms: you always move away from your beloved and back into yourself. The oddity of sex's loneliness is this: a feeling of being unknown when you are most known. One of your most vulnerable and intimate experiences will never satisfy your desire to belong.

$$\left(\begin{array}{c}19\end{array}\right)$$

Mother-Daughter Connections

Does loneliness run in families? If your mother or father was a lonely person, do you have a greater chance of being lonely too? A 2016 study found the tendency to feel lonely over a lifetime (as opposed to feeling lonely occasionally because of one's circumstances) is a modestly heritable trait—14 to 27 percent genetic. This research supports previous studies showing how some of us might be born with a tendency to feel lonelier than others.

Even though it exists, I don't need research to prove loneliness runs in families. I know loneliness runs in families because it runs in my family. My mother, my daughter, and I have all suffered from loneliness in ways that seem uncommon. One day I will forgive my mother for passing this loneliness down to me in the same way she passed down her cheekbones and her hands and her stubbornness. And hopefully one day my daughter will forgive me for passing this trait down to her.

The night my daughter was born, I asked the nurses to keep her in the nursery so I could get some sleep. I had been awake the thirty-six hours leading up to her birth. She was my first baby, and I was exhausted. I had sent my husband and parents home that evening after I ate dinner, because I had planned on sleeping for several hours while the nurses cared for my daughter. Yet each time I handed my tiny, swaddled baby to the nurses for their care, they would soon return her to me because she was too upset. Being with me and nursing were the only things that calmed her.

In the middle of our first night together, exhausted and depleted, I picked up the phone next to my bed to call my mom, who was staying at my house. While cradling my nursing baby in my left arm, I dialed the number for our landline and held the phone to my ear with my right hand. She answered, and through tears, I said, "Mom, I can't get any sleep. Nursing is the only way to keep her from crying."

"Oh, it will be okay," she replied. "Just nurse her as much as you need to tonight, and you can nap when she falls asleep." There was a pause, and then she said, "It will get better." Her words were comforting, because she didn't judge me for wanting to meet my own needs. They were a relief to hear, because they reminded me that the rest I desired wasn't as elusive as it seemed.

A couple hours later the baby quieted and drifted to sleep. I placed her in the bassinet with a terrified gentleness I didn't know existed, climbed back into the bed, and fell asleep, too. When the phone rang early the next morning—a siren wailing into the silence—I woke and lunged across the bed to answer it quickly, worried it would startle the baby. "I'm calling to let you know you called me last night," the woman on the other end of the line said. "You thought I was your mother, and at first I thought you were my daughter. You must have dialed the wrong number. I'm so sorry. I want to make sure you get ahold of your mom." I was stunned, and embarrassed, and moved by her kindness. In a moment of distress, a stranger had provided the comfort I needed.

Indeed glimpses of beauty glisten in this episode: this accidental connection, forged between me and a woman I'd never met, got me through those first wrenching hours of exhaustion. Yet what I remember most about that night was how alone I felt. Holding a distressed newborn and wanting nothing more than to close my eyes and rest: it made me feel like a bad mother, that I was doing everything wrong, that I didn't belong in the circle of good moms who sacrificed sleep to care for their children.

Seventeen years later, as I think back on my first hours of motherhood, I imagine how alone my baby daughter must have felt. Everything in her wanted to be attached to me, to be with me, while I, on the brink of an exhaustion-filled breakdown, kept sending her away.

I imagine the loneliness my own mother might have felt. I, her only daughter, had just given birth to my first child. Perhaps my mother was aware of the way daughters turn slowly away from mothers as they age. Perhaps she knew I would soon be turning away from her in order to turn toward my daughter and my own expanding family.

So here we are, we three, with this heritable trait. These days I try to teach my daughter how to navigate her loneliness. In the same way I have taught her how to navigate self-care and her tendency to fall into black-and-white thinking, I talk through loneliness with her, helping her find her way through its waters to the belonging on the other side.

Maybe I should feel less alone in my loneliness because my mother and my daughter have shared in it. But their knowledge of the weight I bear doesn't lift my own weight. And my knowledge of the weight they bear doesn't lift theirs. Is it possible to divide each other's sorrows when we are all weighed down by the same difficulties? Does this equation have a solution in God's economy?

My Mother's Loneliness

When my mother was a young child living in Cuthbert, Georgia, her best friend was a girl named Beth. Beth's family lived in a house right behind their small town's movie theater. Her father owned a butcher shop that was sandwiched between the movie theater and a pharmacy. When my mother went to Beth's house, they played dress-up and snuck into the pharmacy's dumpster to find discarded makeup samples, including tiny red lipsticks and pale pink blushers they used on their little-girl mouths and round cheeks. They rode their bikes around the neighborhood and roller skated at the temporary rink that came to town for a few weeks every spring. Beth's parents also owned a small motel on the edge of town. Some Friday nights, when Beth's parents were responsible for managing the motel, the girls got to spend the night in one of the rooms. They'd stay up late watching Lucille Ball and Roy Rogers and drinking sodas from the vending machines.

On my mother's last day of third grade, her family moved away from Cuthbert. Heartbroken, because she was leaving Beth and the only place she had ever known, she moved with her family to Clayton, Alabama. And then the following spring, her family moved once again to Shellman, Georgia. My mother's class at her new school was full of kids who had grown up together. She was an outsider when she arrived in Shellman the March of her fourth-grade year, and she remained on the periphery until she left for college.

Another reason my mother felt like an outsider was that she had different aspirations than most of her classmates at Shellman Elementary School and Randolph County Junior High. She knew from a young age that she wanted more than what a typical small-town life could offer. She wanted to go places and experience the things she read about during endless hours at the county library on East Pearl Street. She wanted to attend the theatre and the symphony, and to visit art museums and botanical gardens. She married young—at the age of eighteen, after finishing her first year of college at Auburn University. I've often wondered how my mother's loneliness layered over or underpinned her marriage. Which ways did marriage stitch together the pieces of her loneliness? Perhaps the belonging-to-another that one finds in marriage soothed the isolation she knew so intimately as a child and adolescent. But loneliness exists even in the finest of marriages.

When I was a child, my mother had friends of a sort—wives of my father's colleagues, a few women from the church we attended, neighbors who crossed her path. But she didn't have a friend of the heart. Watching her around other adults, I thought it always seemed like she was holding back, like she was careful to be who they expected her to be.

My mother used to host an open house every Christmas Eve. She put a significant amount of time and effort into decorating our home and cooking and baking food for her guests. One year, after we had moved to a new house in a new neighborhood, no one showed up. Untouched punch bowls and platters of appetizers and holiday cookies spread across the dining table. She sat on the living room sofa, silent and defeated.

I have inherited the attributes responsible for building the scaffolding for my mother's loneliness. I have lived much of my life performing and trying to be the woman, mother, and wife I thought others wanted me to be. I have also been hesitant with many friendships. If it seems like I'm the one doing most of the relational work, most of the pursuing, I move on before I'm rejected. I don't want to be friends with anyone who might skip my party.

After my older brother and I left for college, my parents moved to a new city where my mother formed several meaningful and fulfilling friendships. She now has those friends of the heart who were absent when I was a child, and she rarely struggles with loneliness anymore. I asked her recently about this idea of core loneliness—the kind that transcends circumstance, that is fundamental to the self, that is associated with our longing for heaven and for the "not yet." Even though she now has deep friendships, I thought my mother would at least be familiar with this feeling of core loneliness. She was, and she told me something surprising. "As I've grown older, I've realized I'm already living in eternity," she said. "I see more signs of God's presence here now. It's exciting, and it feels more like an anticipation than a loneliness."

It's an interesting idea—that loneliness is a relative of anticipation. Perhaps they are siblings, showing up for each other and leading each other home.

(21)

Hot Dog Club

When we were in our late twenties, Tim and I were part of a group with many "young marrieds" who founded a church in the Five Points neighborhood of Birmingham. Six years into that ecclesial experiment, the still very tight-knit group of founding couples almost floundered when one of the women, Casey, had an affair and left her husband, David.

I remember a Sunday night when David came over to our house following our church's evening worship service. After we had finished dinner and cleared away the leftovers and the dishes, he crossed his arms on the table in front of him, put his head down, and wept. Tim and I sat with him in silence. We knew there was nothing we could say to make it better.

Casey and David's separation was not the only drama unfolding at our church and the small private school that was connected to it. Fraught relationship dynamics and institutional complexities affected us all in various ways as various things fell apart. I remember it now as a season of great pressure and strain. Some of our friends ran for the doors and found other churches. But Tim and I didn't think it was time to leave our congregation, so we stayed through the turmoil and the questions.

One early summer night, around the time Casey filed for divorce, a small group of us ended up at David's new house to eat hot dogs. One-third the size of the house he and Casey had owned, it was a small, comfortable, brick home with a great backyard. A nice deck welcomed us to stay a while, and empty flower beds along the perimeter called out for someone to care. We ate hot dogs and chips and drank beer outside on the deck while we swatted at the mosquitos and watched the lightning bugs flit around us.

We enjoyed the camaraderie so we met again. And again. Whenever we got together, everyone contributed something—extra-long all-beef franks, extra-long buns, bags of chips, ice cream sandwiches, or beer. David handled the condiments, paper plates, and napkins. Sometimes he surprised us with a warmed-up can of chili or an appetizer of grilled Conecuh sausage.

Most times we gathered, only adults attended. Those of us with kids paid for sitters so we could be present to each other without being interrupted every five seconds—that, and so we could pay more attention to the latest gossip. (It's hard to not gossip when marriages are ending and your church is falling apart.)

Our gatherings had no set schedule. When someone from the group wanted to put dinner on the calendar, they sent an email to all the participants. Then we responded to figure out the date, the time, and who would bring what. During one meal, someone said in between bites, "We should call ourselves the Hot Dog Club." The rest of us agreed.

Our church had been established with the belief that Jesus welcomed the friendless; over the years, those of us in this group had devoted a great deal of energy and time to being available to those who were suffering. We were diligent as we tried to figure out how to minister to the outcasts and the sick. But when everything began to fall apart, we realized *we* were the friendless, the suffering, the outcast, the sick. We needed Jesus to show up for us, too. And he did. He showed up on David's back deck while we gathered in our grief and ate and gossiped and laughed and cried.

I don't remember the last time we met for hot dogs and beer. Whenever it was, I doubt we knew it would be our final gathering. We probably ate, hung out, said our "see you laters," and went our separate ways at the end of the night. Then life happened. Weeks passed. No one sent the next email asking to get together again.

Our lives have since diverged. My family eventually left the church we helped start for a church in a different denomination. David married a wonderful woman who adores him and fills his life with love and their yard with flowers. I hadn't seen or spoken to David in a few years even though we still live in the same city. But a few weeks ago, while I was eating out with a friend, David and his wife appeared at our table. They had just finished their dinner and were on their way to pick up their three girls from her father's house. They stopped to talk to us for a while, and I was so glad to see them. It was a sweet reunion and a beautiful reminder of God's faithfulness to David, and to me, and to all of us.

The other members of the Hot Dog Club have all moved away now. I'm still in touch with them—some to a greater degree than others. I wish we could all gather again and talk about that season of turmoil—how God gave us to each other, and how faithful God has been to us since those days. I wish we could talk about how God had sorted through the shattered pieces of our lives and put them back together again.

$$\binom{22}{}$$

Buddy Benches

A group of second graders at an elementary school in Portsmouth, Ohio, petitioned their superintendent to create "buddy benches" for their school's playgrounds. The benches, which were installed in the spring of 2019, help students connect with each other during recess. When someone sits on a buddy bench, classmates know to approach the student and ask if they want to talk or play. Reflecting on the benches, one second grader said, "It's to make sure you always have someone there for you if you are going through a hard time."

Around the same time, detective Ashley Jones found himself in conversations with lonely people of all ages in his precinct in western England. People sometimes told him they were lonely and might go days or weeks without talking to another person. An older woman he spoke with described why she had been scammed out of a large sum of money by a stranger. The thief called her on the phone every morning, preying on her isolation and pretending to be her friend. She eventually sent him more than thirty thousand dollars because she thought she was helping someone who cared about her.

Jones was alarmed by the way loneliness had exacerbated this woman's vulnerability to theft. So Jones and his police department added "chat benches" to parks in the area. He hoped the benches would encourage more interaction between residents in his community. He attached signs to the first two designated chat benches with a message saying, "The 'Happy to chat' bench. Sit here if you don't mind someone stopping to say hello." A few days later, Jones took walks by both benches and found people sitting and talking to each other.

As news of the chat benches spread, people in other areas of England and in other countries made plans to create designated chat benches as well. Jones said, "All who participate gain a positive outcome from getting involved. The chat bench removes that invisible social barrier that prevents people from saying 'hello.'" Police officers and other municipal leaders are discovering how greater social cohesion improves their residents' sense of wellbeing, reduces their isolation, and makes them less susceptible to scams.

Perhaps we need to learn from the Portsmouth students and the British detective, and place buddy benches and chat benches all over our neighborhoods. We could put them in coffee shops, libraries, corporate offices, churches, and on street corners. These benches seem to address personal loneliness—"I feel lonely"—*and* social alienation—"We don't know our neighbors." They extend an invitation to individuals who want to interact with others and provide a starting place for those who may not feel lonely but want to help build social cohesion in their communities. The benches offer hope for a new reality where people hold fast to two truths: we all belong, and we all belong to each other.

$$\left(\begin{array}{c}23\end{array}\right)$$

A Chance Encounter

On a bright fall morning, I drove down First Avenue North from my home on the eastern end of Birmingham toward downtown. I made my way to a new urban park that was to officially open the following day. I wanted to check it out before the crowds swarmed the highly publicized addition to our city. My kids were at school and my husband was at work, so I went alone to see what I could see.

After I found a parking spot on the street, I grabbed my blanket, book, and water bottle and approached a walking path encircling nineteen acres of green space containing a large open lawn, hundreds of trees, and patches of flowers. A lake, ponds, and streams shimmered in the sunshine. Teens on skateboards congregated in nearby skate bowls. The sound of plastic wheels on concrete brought to mind childhood memories of roller skates and Big Wheel trikes. It was an unlikely oasis in the middle of a bustling business district, and I felt like a character from a fairy tale stepping into a secret land.

I found a place to lay out my blanket, but I was too buzzed to read. The energy and beauty of the space produced a joy in me, and I wanted to it share with others. Apparently I wasn't the only person with this response, because within minutes of sitting down, I was approached by an older gentleman. "Can you believe this?" he asked, spreading his arms wide and gesturing toward the space.

"It's beautiful," I responded. "I wasn't sure what to expect, but seeing it for the first time startled me." My new acquaintance and I introduced ourselves, and then I stood so we could continue chatting. What neighborhood do you live in? How long have you been in Birmingham? How do you think this place will change the city?

He told me about his grandchildren and how much he loved to cook. He and his wife and several of his buddies threw elaborate tailgating parties at a local university's home football games. "You and your family should join us!" he said. "I'm grilling ribs at the next game. You really don't want to miss out on my ribs," he said with a wink.

We didn't make it to the party the following Saturday, so we missed out on his famous ribs. I later lost track of his phone number, but I never lost track of the memory of our encounter. It's where it's supposed to be—dangling on the corner of my delight.

Whenever I visit the park, I wonder if I'll run into him. I wonder about his oldest grandson, who planned to be the first from his family to go to college. I wonder about his wife and his friends and the delicious food they might be preparing for the next time they're all together. And I wonder if he remembers meeting me at our city's new park when we had plenty of space to connect, to belong.

24

Coffee Shop Company

When I arrive at a local coffee shop after dropping my kids off at school on a Tuesday morning in April, I am pleased to find my favorite table empty. The one table constructed of real wood is stationed across from the pastry case and next to a shelf full of memoirs and history books. Sitting there means I can nestle up to a bay window that has a lovely view of trees with spring-green leaves and a clock tower topped with a spire and with Roman numerals marking each hour. After several days of clouds and rain, the sky is a bright, sun-soaked blue.

My favorite table is a decent size, not too big, not too small. Goldilocks would approve. Four chairs are crowded around it this morning, and I wonder how comfortable this arrangement was for the table's previous occupants. It could legitimately be a table for one if, with a certain studious intentionality, you spread a lot of notebooks and papers across the surface. But it's really more of a table for two. It may work for three people if everyone knows each other well, and it only seats four comfortably if you pull it away from the wall and place one of the chairs on that side by the window.

After parking my bag and computer at my favorite table, and before ordering a medium coffee, I move one of the four chairs to another table. I don't want to hog a table for four, but I can get by with hogging a table for three if I place my bag in the first chair, sit in the second, and leave the third empty. When everything is settled, I sit down and begin writing. Twenty minutes later, a man sits down in the empty chair directly across from me. So many other tables in the shop are empty. He doesn't even ask if he can join me. He doesn't say a word.

Apparently I won't be hogging a table after all.

He places his laptop in front of him and removes the packaging from a new power cord. "I can plug that in for you," I offer, since the outlet is in the wall beside my chair. I'm proud of myself for engaging this stranger and pretending I'm not shocked by his actions.

"Thank you. I appreciate it," he responds.

We make no further eye contact. He's wearing a taupe V-neck sweater over a blue and white checked button-down shirt. His head full of dark hair makes him appear younger than the lines of his face suggest. His glasses, earbuds, and keys are on the table beside his computer.

Soon he walks over to a corner at the other end of the shop. Two men with clerical collars who arrived a few minutes ago are having coffee together. He shakes their hands and says, "Nice to see you!" before returning to his seat. At my table. My favorite table.

Now he is on his phone, speaking a language other than English. I wish I knew which language he is speaking. I wish I knew why he chose to sit at my favorite table. Why does he think this is okay?

Then again, I wish I knew why I am so concerned with his actions. I return to my writing, but I can't quit thinking about my new tablemate. Why is this bothering me so much?

Now he's leaving. He asks me to unplug his cord, I hand it to him, and he places it in his brown leather bag along with his computer. We exchange goodbyes. He walks out the door.

A few minutes later, I ask the shop's owner if he knows the man who was sitting with me. "No. I thought you were helping him with writing or something," he says. "Do you not know him?"

"Nope. I've never seen him."

We exchange puzzled looks and shoulder shrugs. Maybe my favorite table was simply my tablemate's favorite table, too. Or he needed to be near the sunlight. Or he didn't want to be alone.

(25)

'Tis the Season

It's the first Sunday of Advent—the beginning of a new church year, the start of the season designed to draw me into the story of God's loving provision. I wake while my husband and children are still sleeping. Early weekend mornings are my favorite mornings, because they give me extended time alone to read, write, and pray. I usually check social media, too, but the previous night I had decided Sundays would be social media–free for me. I want to refrain from Twitter, Facebook, and Instagram on Sundays until sundown. I want to enter more fully into the Sabbath, and one way to do that is to put a moratorium on scrolling through photos, opinions, news bites, memes, and cat videos.

I walk down the hall to the kitchen table where an Advent wreath sits in the center, a circle of greenery and candles nestled into a foamy floral oasis. I light a purple candle for the first Sunday of Advent. Then I grab my phone and snap a photo.

I can't help it. Well, I can help it, but I don't want to help it. For some reason, being alone feels too lonely. Maybe if other people were aware of where I am and what I'm doing, and if they approved of me being where I am and what I'm doing, I might feel less isolated. Or more distracted from my isolation.

I edit the image of the burning candle. First, I crop it to remove the background distractions threatening to draw an observer's eye away from the photo's focus. Then I open Instagram and apply the "slumber" filter because it most distinctly displays the candle's flame. I post the picture, along with a caption including the Collect for the First Sunday of Advent, Rite One from the Book of Common Prayer. I share an identical post on Facebook, where I also insert a statement that I will be off social media for the rest of the day. If anyone needs me, they can email or text. The post shows my home, my faith, and my self as I want them to appear: my home as clean, warm, and inviting; my faith as lovely, calm, and rooted in the liturgical year; my self as disciplined and free from the reign of social media.

I pour a mug of coffee and sit down at the table, basking in the glow of that one purple candle. While I write in my journal and contemplate this season of waiting for Jesus's arrival, my phone notifies me of Instagram and Facebook likes. Several of my friends, as well as people I don't know and will never meet, approve my message. And bursts of dopamine distract me from my loneliness and lure me into thinking I'm seen and known.

A List of Lost Friends
and Answered Prayers

1. She lived down the street from me and we attended the same preschool. She loved horses, the Dallas Cowboy Cheerleaders, and the *Grease* soundtrack. We put on her mom's high heels and lipstick and stumbled and tumbled throughout her house. Whenever we pretended to be mothers or teachers, she stirred up conflict and drama. I only wanted peace and harmony.

2. We made necklaces and crowns of weeds and pretended to be bothered when boys chased us around the dry, dusty playground. After she moved three hours south, following second grade, we visited each other's homes for a couple of summers. When I stayed with her family, we were responsible for cleaning the apartment every day before her mom and stepdad came home from work. Another task was to prepare the coffeemaker for their evening coffee so they would only have to push a button. Every day

we washed the glass carafe, added enough water for two servings to the chamber, filled the paper filter with scoops of ground coffee beans, and, to my wonder, added a few shakes of salt and pepper.

3. She was my best friend in junior high, when I was old enough to think we'd be friends forever. We hosted our thirteenth birthday parties together around a swimming pool with a DJ and chicken fingers and a sheet cake. We listened to James Taylor, The Eagles, and the *Stand by Me* soundtrack late into the night whenever I slept over at her house. Our friendship wasn't done until after we both got married, but it had been fading for so long.

4. She was the maid of honor in my wedding. After she moved away, we prayed together on the phone every week. We prayed for our husbands. We prayed for our babies. We prayed for our attitudes. Then I got sick and it became too much to pray and talk and fill her in on my mania and my depression and how hard motherhood was for me while I was manic and depressed. Too much time passed. I didn't call her back, and she eventually stopped trying.

5. She led a discipleship group of young, newly married women. We met once every week for three years. She told us sin caused depression. I was depressed at the time, but didn't know it. Well, maybe I knew I was depressed—at least on some level— because I kept repenting over and over again for my lack of contentment. More praying for husbands. More praying for babies. More praying for attitudes. Then I started going to a new church, and my perspective on discipleship and community began to shift. I left her group, and she and I drifted apart. I ran into her several years later, and we exchanged polite hellos.

6. She taught me about beauty and longing. She inspired me to speak up, to use my voice, to value my role as a woman in the church. Then I became one of many women who used to be her friend. I joined the multitude of those she had cast aside and those who saw the truth of her character and stepped back on their own accord. We were a trail of crumbs pointing to what used to be.

7. She was my best friend when I was finally old enough to know best friends don't last forever. My two bouts of severe mania and depression were hard for her. Then she moved. She and her husband came to town for New Year's Eve a few years ago. We ate dates stuffed with goat cheese and wrapped in bacon. We drank champagne. We laughed with our husbands while we ushered in a new year, a new start. But I haven't seen her since.

• • •

A few months ago, I told my spiritual director I felt disconnected from people. I was alone too much, and some weeks I only saw my husband and our kids. My few dear friends at the time were in busy seasons. "Maybe I need more friends," I said.

"You could pray about it," she responded. "Ask God to meet you in this. Ask for more friends."

Susan always notices what's going on beneath my words. She's about ten years older than I am, with gorgeous shoulder-length gray hair and a calm, soothing demeanor. She's easy to talk to, and she listens well. I should have figured out this plan of action on my own, but I am forgetful and full of doubt and need my spiritual director to remind me to turn to God in times of distress.

I know I should pray about things such as my desire for more friends. But asking God for specific personal requests—things I really want—is sometimes hard for me. I pray for my husband, my kids, my friends, my family, my neighbors, my city, my country, my world. But most of my prayers don't use words. I usually practice centering prayer, which is a fancy way to say I sit quietly with God.

Even though I pray, prayer confuses me if I think too much about it. I appreciate what Rowan Williams writes in *Being Christian*: "I may not quite know what is going on; as prayer deepens in me I am less and less likely to know what is going on. I may be baffled, I may be depressed, and I may feel that absolutely nothing is happening: fine. Just stay there and if in doubt say, 'O God, make speed to save me.'" Sometimes that's the extent of my prayer: *O God, make speed to save me.*

But during this meeting with my spiritual director, asking God for new friends sounded like a great idea. I was lonely enough to pray for more friends. I was desperate enough to hope for a different future. I became a child who still believed her wishes could come true. So with my usual sense of things related to faith—not knowing what is going on but doing it anyway—I prayed and asked God for more friends. And within days I received what I had asked for.

Honestly. I don't know how it worked. I only know I prayed for a specific thing for myself, and God answered in the way I wanted. I didn't even have to initiate these potential friendships—I just had to receive and respond. A neighbor invited me to meet for coffee. "I'd love to meet for coffee." A priest from my church asked if Tim and I could help lead a small group. "Of course!" An acquaintance I hadn't seen in years asked me to lunch. "Lunch sounds great!"

I know it sounds improbable, and maybe too simple. Maybe my prayers made me more open to friendship, lifting the veil of solitude to reveal potential friends who were already hovering around me in the shadows. Or maybe it was all a coincidence. Or it's a mystery I'll never understand. Whatever it was, I'm grateful.

• • •

1. We were found by each other in our suffering. We showed up again and again. We stayed.

2. We met for coffee one summer morning and kept meeting for coffee through autumn, winter, and spring. We're in the same small group now so we see each other most Sunday nights. We converse in hushed voices. "You too?" we say. "Yes. Me too."

3. She and her husband bought our house when we moved to a new neighborhood. She told me she wanted to be my friend. Now we sit on her front porch (my old front porch) and share in each other's sorrows and joys. We talk about life and death and faith. We sit in silence while we wait for the trains to pass, horns and steel on steel, rumbling and roaring.

4. We connected on social media, and it's a bit of a miracle that we found each other amid all of those zeroes and ones. They are writers and mothers who are around my age. We trade essays and messages and emails. They live many miles away, and we haven't been friends for long. I know some of our friendships will flourish and some won't. And that's okay.

5. She's a friend I lost and then found again more than twenty years later. We are both so different now. We inhabit the gray spaces with blurred boundaries. We have fewer answers and more questions.

6. We first connected through our words. I wish she would write more. I'm always encouraging her to write more. She and her husband live in Germany now so we communicate via messages that usually arrive while we are sleeping. We often remind each other we are okay, we will be okay, God has us.

We Sing to Belong

When three Minneapolis choral groups gathered in 2016 to rehearse and perform *The Voyage*, one of their primary aims was to alleviate loneliness through creating a sense of community. The performance of *The Voyage*, sung by a combined choir of members aged nine to ninety, used music to explore feelings stirred by the aging process. While writing the words for the chorale, librettist Charles Bennett found inspiration in the various stages of life, how we encounter voids we need to cross, from childhood to adolescence to adulthood to senescence. "The voyage on one level is the way that we move through time . . . or perhaps the way that time moves through us," Bennett explained. He wanted the lyrics to rouse the performers and listeners and produce within them a sense of yearning and joyful connection.

During rehearsals, choir director G. Phillip Shoultz asked the group questions such as "Have you ever known anyone who's dealt with mental illness?" and "Have you ever felt isolated or alone?"

to encourage the singers to open up with each other. One of the choir participants sent Shoultz an email and shared these thoughts:

> When we were split into groups and you asked the question, "Have you ever felt so lonely that you isolated yourself from others?" I remember feeling nervous to step forward. . . . I was surprised to see most in the room step forward, including the younger kids. . . . [T]o know that everyone struggles with this and seeing young and old step forward, was incredibly powerful to me. I kept looking at the kids in my group and wondered how they felt, whether they felt the same warm sense of connection that I felt, whether they felt less isolated in their own lives—I hope so.

Even if you're not in a choir whose director knits you together with intimate questions, singing in a group can make you feel bonded and connected to other people. One study found that "older adults who sang in [a] community choir experienced significantly less perceived social isolation and more 'interest in life.'" I imagine this is true for community singers of all ages.

But scholars haven't solved all of the riddles of musically alleviated loneliness. Exactly *how* does singing in a community choir help people feel less isolated? Is it the act of singing? Is it singing with other people? A bit of both?

I'm not in a choir, but when I sing at church on Sunday mornings, I have a greater sense of belonging than when I don't—even though I only know a dozen of the people in the room with me. So I'm inclined to think singing-and-belonging can't be reduced to, say, the community-building that can occur through weekly rehearsals with other singers. Maybe the actual engagement of my voice and auditory function help me feel less lonely. Maybe the words I sing help me feel less lonely too.

During a recent worship service, we sang one of my favorite hymns, "From the Depths of Woe," a song I first encountered in church about twenty years ago. The hymn, based on Psalm 130, was written by Martin Luther in 1523, six years after the beginning of the Protestant Reformation. I've typically sung the lyrics set to music that was written in the 1990s by Christopher Miner. When Indelible Grace Music recorded Miner's version of the song for one of their albums, they set the first two verses in a minor key and then the music transitions to a major key for the rest of the song. Describing Indelible Grace's decision to record the hymn in this way, Kevin Twit wrote:

> So often our experience here and now is a cry from the depths of woe, and we mustn't minimize the reality of that place that God's people regularly experience. And there is a certain comfort that comes from singing together in that place, we are not alone, and song can help us experience this. But there is real hope for those who trust in Jesus—there is a joy beyond the sorrow, a day when God will set His Israel free from all her sin and sorrow. Yet you don't easily or quickly go from the depths of woe to trusting with joy. I love the way this hymn takes five verses (and seven minutes) to make the journey.

The cries for God's mercy and proclamations of faith in "From the Depths of Woe" always seem appropriate for me to sing, whatever my condition or circumstance. Singing this hymn always reminds me of who I have become, who God has formed me to be. It reminds me of God's faithfulness over the years since I first uttered the song's first lines:

> From the depths of woe, I raise to Thee
> The voice of lamentation;
> Lord, turn a gracious ear to me
> And hear my supplication

I have known many depths of much woe over the past two decades. I have known much lament. But God has offered me a gracious ear and heard my supplication. When I sing "From the Depths of Woe," I think about the church at which I learned the song, a church my family eventually left. I think about what we held and what we let go when we decided to leave this church and its people. I think about all of this and sing the verses crafted to carry me along from sorrow to thanksgiving, and I start crying. Every single time. Because it's impossible for me to sing while I'm crying, it's been years since I've sung this hymn in its entirety.

Singing is a communal act. This is obvious when we are performing with choirs or singing at church on Sundays. It's not so obvious when we sing a hymn alone in our cars on a Tuesday afternoon while running errands. But I believe my off-key, butchered rendition of "From the Depths of Woe" when I'm on my way home from the grocery store is also a communal act. It connects me to others who have sung the hymn throughout the ages. It connects me to God and reminds me who God is and who God will always be.

$$\left(\begin{array}{c}28\end{array}\right)$$

All the Saints

I enter the nave of an Episcopal church right before the service begins. The others in attendance are seated in the chancel, the space at the front of the church where the choir usually sits during worship. I slip into the end of a pew beside a man I don't know, surrounded by others I don't know. I am younger than most of those present. I face a dozen or so women and one man who appear to be in their fifties and sixties in the pews opposite mine.

The lights are dimmed, but the afternoon sun shines through stained-glass windows. Three windows on the wall in front of me depict scenes from Jesus's life and ministry. A tall, brass candelabra in the center of the wooden chancel floor holds a single white candle, its flame burning. The organist plays a prelude. No one stirs.

For three years, I've been a member of a larger Episcopal church downtown, but in the last several months, I've been coming to this smaller church near my house for weekday morning prayer, and I was happy to learn they were observing All Saints'

Day. I've never been to a weekday All Saints' Day service. At my church, on the Sunday after All Saints' we sometimes sing "For All the Saints" and read a list of those who have died in the past year during the regular prayer time. So here I am, at three o'clock on a Friday afternoon, in the company of strangers, honoring those who have entered heaven.

In the few minutes before the priest calls us into the presence of God, I calm myself from the rush to get here and begin to think of people I knew who died in the past year. I remember a third cousin, Bobby, who was my father's age and whose family showed me hospitality during the two summers I attended summer school after my freshman and sophomore years of college. Bobby and his wife, Carol, graciously invited me into their home and the life of their family. They made extra coffee every morning and welcomed me at dinnertime, which was always at six o'clock. I often joined them and their two sons for the nourishing meals Carol had prepared, but I was free to skip if I had other plans or wanted to be alone.

I also remember a writer I followed on Twitter and with whom I'd exchanged a few emails. Whenever I engaged her on social media or through our one-on-one correspondence—even when I disagreed with her—she was always kind. She helped me consider theological issues from different angles. She had a significant affect on many Christians, and her tragic death has caused much grief for those who knew her well and those who only knew her through her words.

I remember others, and I wonder who I'm forgetting. I wish I had given this more thought before now. The priest calls us to worship and then reads the Collect for All Saints' from the Book of Common Prayer:

> Almighty God, who hast knit together thine elect in one fellowship in the mystical body of thy Son Christ our Lord: Give us grace to follow thy blessed saints in all virtuous and godly living, that we may come to those ineffable joys that thou hast prepared for those who unfeignedly love thee; through the same Jesus Christ our Lord, who with thee and the Holy Spirit liveth and reigneth, one God, in glory everlasting. *Amen.*

The words are pleasing to my ear. I love the sound, and the hope, of "that we may come to those ineffable joys that thou hast prepared for those who unfeignedly love thee." The rhythm and diction of the Collect, in addition to its meaning and purpose, give me comfort. Its truth soothes me because those I remember—and those I've forgotten—now know the ultimate fulfillment of those ineffable joys.

During one of the hymns, we sing, "Who are these like stars appearing, these, before God's throne who stand? Each a golden crown is wearing; who are all this glorious band? Alleluia! Hark, they sing, praising loud their heavenly King." I adore this hymn and can't help but think about theologian Fleming Rutledge's response when she's asked why she has stayed in the Episcopal church even though her theology bends more conservative than that of the denomination's leadership. Whenever she is asked this question, which happens often, she always says something like this: "The Episcopal Hymnal, which I snootily think is the best among those of all of the churches (and I have seen most of them)."

After the Gospel reading, we pray for all saints. I think the priest is saying, in alphabetical order, the names of those who have died over the past year. But when he gets to the *b*'s I become anxious because this is taking longer than I anticipated and I'm kneeling and I think my quads might give out. I mean, he's got the rest of the alphabet ahead of him! Then I glance at my order of worship and I realize it's going to be even longer than I thought. We are praying for every person who has died since this church was started . . . in 1887.

I look to the left and notice the others on my pew are no longer on the kneelers and instead are seated, with their torsos bowed. I join them, quiet my distracted mind, and give my attention to the priest's voice and the cadence of the names of the saints. I have never met any of those being remembered. A few sound familiar, as their surnames are those of influential families in this city—Jemison and Yielding. Several of those read in succession share the same last name. They are spouses, or parents and their children, or grandparents and their children and their children's children—several generations of families who worshiped in this place. I make the names into a breath prayer. I inhale as the priest says a name. I exhale with the next. Inhale. Exhale. Inhale. Exhale.

I have known about the Communion of Saints since I was a young child reciting the Apostles' Creed every Sunday, my voice mingling with the voices of my mother, my father, my brother, and others seated near us. But I didn't give it much thought until I was older, more mature in my faith, and more aware of the church year. When I noticed All Saints' Day occurred every November 1 and how we usually sang "For All the Saints" the following Sunday, I began to think more about what it means to be a part of the larger church. I began to envision myself as connected to all Christians who have died and to all who have not yet been born.

The theology of the Communion of Saints sustains me when I am too sick, too full of doubt, or too disappointed to believe. I read words written by the psalmists, the apostles, Teresa of Avila, Thomas Cranmer, Anne Lamott, Rowan Williams, and others, and I know their moments of faith carry me when I'm unable to travel the road of faith on my own. I listen to those around me on Sunday mornings when we all recite the prayers, creeds, and confessions in one voice, and I know I'm not alone in my faith or my failures. My prayers ferry others when my ability to believe is less deterred than theirs. And their prayers ferry me. I watch friends, acquaintances, and strangers walk forward for the Eucharist. Then I eat from the same loaf and drink from the same cup that have satisfied their hunger and quenched their thirst.

The more I think about the Communion of Saints, the more it makes sense to me that I attend an All Saints' Day service at a church of which I am not a member. When I'm sitting among strangers and listening to the names of strangers, I'm more in tune with our commonality, which transcends relational ties. And I'm more in tune to our union made possible by our triune God—the One to whom we all belong and the One who provides that for which we all search.

$$\left(29 \right)$$

Giving Away What We Want Most

I sat in a spacious living room decorated in soothing teals, creams, and whites while I listened to a theologian and seminary professor. We were in a home of a friend—a woman who had welcomed me into her life and opened my eyes to the significance of beauty and wonder and creating welcoming spaces for others. The man speaking was one of her mentors, so I listened with an eager attention. He talked about the importance of the hearth and the home.

I don't remember many details from his talk, but here's what I do remember. I remember his thinning gray hair, his black trousers, his simple white button-down shirt. I remember his British accent and his eyes that seemed capable of seeing through me. When he finished speaking to the small group assembled, I approached him and asked if he had any thoughts on how to develop stronger connections with other Christians. I told him

I wanted more meaningful friendships and asked what I should do. He looked at me and said, "Give people what you want the most." He said if I want meaningful friendships with others, I could aim to be a good friend. If I want others to include me, I should aim to include others. If I want to be cared for and loved, I could aim to care for and love others.

This way of interacting can be difficult. It requires vulnerability, and for me to know what I want. Sometimes I try to meet others in ways I wanted to be met during previous seasons of life. One morning I visited with my friend in her home as she held her newborn son. He was so tiny and had severe health issues. I could sense her sadness and a bit of hesitation as a new mother. I told her what I had wanted someone to tell me when my first child was a newborn: "It's okay if you don't feel completely in love with your baby yet," I said. "It took me a few weeks to get to know Riley after she was born and to feel the intense love that some mothers say they experience immediately. I felt so guilty at first. But then a few weeks into it, we connected. I felt deep love like none I had ever known. Maybe I needed some sleep. Maybe we needed time nursing and bonding. But I learned motherhood doesn't look the same for all of us. So it's okay if it takes some time."

Right now, I'm staying with a friend in another town for a few days to care for their young son and to help her and her husband have a bit of freedom and time together. They're coming out of a difficult and traumatic season. While I can't empathize with precisely what they have been through the past few months, I can imagine what I would want if I were in their situation. I would want time to reconnect with my husband, process what we had been through, and hope together for a different future.

I haven't always been able to give this friend what I have wanted. During another hard time in her life, I was manic and sick and unable to show up for her. I was stuck in bed, drugged. Then when her son was born, I was unable to be present or help her because I was experiencing my own significant parenting stress. At the time I couldn't leave my own family to be with her. I couldn't give her what I would have wanted the most.

But now I'm here with her son while he watches one of his favorite movies. I fed him a dinner of rice and beans, green peas, and chopped tomato on a bright orange plate. I gave him a small pack of cookies when he finished, and a cup of what he calls "ice cold milk." And in a little while, I will give him a bath, help him into his pajamas, and listen to him tell me about everyone who keeps him safe.

Giving others what I most want doesn't guarantee I will receive anything in return, but it does ease my loneliness. The next time I feel lonely, I want to remember to give someone else what I want most. Lord, help me remember.

Part III

BELONGING TO OUR PLACES

$$\left(30\right)$$

Five Points

On September 15, 1995, I was with my friend Reed at an ice cream shop in Five Points Circle, Birmingham. The five-point star, where two roads intersect and another branches off, is the bustling heart of the Five Points South neighborhood, which is filled with restaurants, bars, and shops.

Reed is one year younger than I am, and at the time we were both students at Birmingham-Southern College. She had a steadiness about her. She wasn't riding any roller coasters like I was—the ones that soared high and dipped low depending on my circumstances, my grades, and which boys noticed me (or didn't). She talked about her relationship with God like it was normal, and she pretended I knew what she was talking about. She didn't beat me over the head (figuratively or literally, thank goodness) with her Bible. She was kind and curious. She was a friend to me, and in the process, she showed me what it meant to be a Christian.

Reed and other Christians I knew had something I didn't have. They didn't seem to be as lonely as I was. They belonged to a sort of Jesus club, and I was on the outside. I had gone to church my whole life, but I didn't know being a Christian involved more than showing up on Sunday mornings in a fancy dress. Much of the preaching I had heard emphasized how to be a good person, which was fine when I was younger, because I thought I measured up. But during college, I left church every week feeling worse than I felt when I arrived. I knew I wasn't a good person—how I used my time on Friday and Saturday nights was proof. And while I didn't always understand everything my Christian friends said about God and Jesus, I had a feeling that if I could have what Reed had, I could stop riding those roller coasters.

While Reed was telling me about a recent argument she had with her boyfriend, I stopped her mid-sentence. "I don't think I've ever accepted Jesus as my savior," I blurted. "Is that how you say it? I've always gone to church because it was what I was supposed to do, but I've never understood my need for Jesus. I can't be perfect. I'm sinful. It all makes sense now. I tried so hard for so long to be someone I can't be. What do I do?"

Reed looked at me with her huge eyes that always seemed to sparkle (would Jesus make my eyes sparkle?) and told me I didn't need to do anything else. She prayed with me right there outside the ice cream shop, under the glow of Five Points streetlights, in the presence of many unknowing witnesses who were busy eating their rocky road ice cream or strawberry sorbet.

After we said, "Amen," I felt lighter. Really. I had tried to help myself for so long. When I realized my efforts to be a good person were futile, I had rebelled in every way possible. I hadn't been able to help myself, and my rebellion had only made me more miserable. It was finally time to give all of it up. After I prayed with Reed, I could breathe more easily. I felt a true sense of freedom for the first time since childhood, when I'd had few worries beyond which cartoons to watch on Saturday mornings.

I still remember the gravity of the first night when everything about the gospel made sense. It was my legitimate moment of saving grace. My spiritual Rubik's Cube was finally solved. After I had turned and twisted the pieces of my life for so many years, trying to fit them where they didn't belong and figure out the winning method or solution or answer, Someone Else solved the puzzle. Every piece was where it was supposed to be, and there was nothing I could do to mess it up. It was finished.

I immediately knew God was involved in every detail of my life and had been all along. When I went back to my dorm room and read my Bible, the words made sense and were no longer a jumbled mix of undecipherable code. I started with the Gospel of Matthew and was able to follow the storyline for the first time. I gobbled up Scripture like it was the only bread capable of satisfying my hunger. I prayed too, with prayers full of thanks to God for loving and forgiving me.

I also felt closer to Reed and other Christian women in my life. It was as if they were standing in a circle holding hands, and when they saw me, they made space for me to join their circle. I was part of something bigger than myself, and I liked it. Being a Christian soothed my loneliness. I belonged in the Jesus club, too.

Five years later, after graduating from college and getting married, my husband and I joined dozens of people at a new church that met in the Pickwick building in Five Points. We didn't have real church services at first, because our pastor didn't want to scare away anyone who wasn't sure about the whole church scene. No music. No sacraments. Just our pastor talking about his hopes and ideas and how we would be a church for the city—a church for the friendless, the sorrowing, and the poor.

The first official worship service with music, a sermon, and Communion took place a few months after the launch group started meeting. Our pastor stood up front in the center, and the musicians were over to the side. He was tall and slim with dark hair that was beginning to gray. There were no vestments. He wore jeans with an untucked shirt.

A table in front of him held bread and wine. When the music started, our voices joined to sing old hymns—some we knew from previous churches, others that were very old and obscure. One of my favorite songs during the church's early days was "Ten Thousand Times Ten Thousand" written by Henry Alford in the 1800s. When we sang the third verse, it was hard to not think about where we came from and where we were going:

> O then what raptured greetings on Canaan's happy
>   shore;
> What knitting severed friendships up, where partings
>   are no more!
> Then eyes with joy shall sparkle, that brimmed with
>   tears of late;
> Orphans no longer fatherless, nor widows desolate.

Our pastor preached about suffering and disappointment and how the truths of the gospel permeate every area of our lives. "The gospel changes everything," he repeated every week. We took notes back then. Many of us were young and grasped onto theology with every tool available, including our pens and paper. If we took notes during the sermon, surely it increased the odds of some of it sinking deeper into our hearts and minds and souls.

After the sermon we sang another hymn—a song of thanksgiving—and then our pastor led us in the liturgy for Communion, which he called the Holy Feast. He picked up the bread, tore it in half, and held both pieces high so we could see. "This is my body, which is for you. Do this in remembrance of me." He lifted a goblet above his head. "This cup is the new covenant in my blood. Do this, as often as you drink it, in remembrance of me."

Then we gathered around the table. He gave us pieces of bread and offered us the cup to drink. We chewed the body and drank the blood. The taste of wine lingered in our mouths as we went home with high hopes.

Tim and I thought we would be in this church and with its people for our remaining days. The church wasn't perfect, but it was good. After a couple of years, many of us from the church made the decision to move into the city from the suburbs we had lived in since we all got married. Tim and I bought a house near Five Points and became friends with our neighbors. We developed meaningful relationships with other people from our church and discussed life and faith and mercy and justice. My sense of loneliness was at an all-time low. I thought we would all grow old together.

But those plans were thwarted. Our pastor created a church

that was safe for people who were struggling, doubting, and falling apart; then about six years in, he struggled, doubted, and fell apart. During the earthquake responsible for rattling our church's foundation, our pastor left his wife, left our church, and married the former wife of one of his former elders.

While we were feeling some of the earthquake's early foreshocks, our church left the building in Five Points where my faith was transformed, where both of my kids were baptized, where I first thought about what it means to love the city, care for the oppressed, and welcome the friendless. We moved to a building a couple of miles away with more room for childcare and a larger worship space. Several years later, when we could still sense some of the lingering aftershocks, my family left that church.

When I was suffering from mania during my second big manic episode during June of 2011, when I had no business driving a car, I drove to the Starbucks in Five Points. We had moved from our house near Five Points a few years before and now lived ten minutes away, on the east side of the city. After I managed to arrive in one piece, I bought an iced latte, sat at a table outside in the June sunshine, and watched the activity around me. I could see the patio of the former ice cream shop where I sat with Reed. I could see the building where I once worshipped.

Because of my mania, I was euphoric. The sun was bright and seemed more awake. The sky was clear—it bathed itself in the bluest of blues. All of the colors on the buildings and signs were bolder, like dancers on a stage basking in their spotlights. There was a photo waiting to be taken everywhere I looked, so I snapped several pictures with my iPhone.

Then Tommy appeared at my table. Tommy lived in the area and attended the church in the early years when we met in the Pickwick building. He was a kind man who also suffered from mental illness and was unable to remember my name. But he knew my face.

"Hey, Christine," he said as he settled into a chair next to me.

"Hi, Tommy. How are you?"

"I'm still here."

"I'm not surprised at all to see you're still here."

"How's the church. How's the pastor?"

"Well, a lot has changed," I said. "He stopped being our pastor soon after we moved to the new building. And he died about a month ago after a short battle with pancreatic cancer. I'm sorry you're just now finding out."

Tommy didn't respond immediately but looked directly into my eyes for several seconds. While he held my gaze, I was worried he could see inside my mind or detect the essence of my illness. But maybe he was remembering the kindness our former pastor had shown him, how he invited the whole church to celebrate Tommy's birthday every year with a big sheet cake. He finally spoke as he stood to leave. "Bye, Christine. See you later." Tommy walked away, and I returned to my photos.

The space where the ice cream shop once sat is currently vacant. Various businesses occupy our former church's original home in the Pickwick building. My family occasionally ventures into Five Points to eat barbecue or Thai food or pancakes at restaurants in the area. I always look for Tommy when we're in the neighborhood, but I can never see him.

(31)

Home Sweet Home

I walked into our former home's living room, through the dining room, and entered the bright kitchen, with its white cabinets and black-and-white checkerboard ceramic tile. It was comforting to feel the familiar incline of the floor, which slanted down from one side of the room to the other. When my husband and I renovated this kitchen, the man who did our tile work told us it wasn't necessary to make it level, and we were trusting enough to take his word for it. We had a contract on the house within a few days of listing it for sale, so I guess the new owner didn't mind either.

"I'm so sorry we left all of this here," I said. "Thanks for letting me pick it up. This stuff is expensive to replace," I told her, as I bent down and grabbed the blue plastic tub of cleaning supplies out from under the sink. I stood up and looked out the window, and the permanence of our move from our first house suddenly hit me. Hard. This was the last time I would look out this window onto this front yard. I started weeping. It was sudden and uncontrollable. The dam broke, and my tears flowed. I could barely breathe or speak.

I managed to make it to the living room and eased myself down onto the brick fireplace hearth. Placing the bucket of cleaning supplies on the wood floor beside me, I put my face in my hands, embarrassed and ashamed. When I could form words, I apologized over and over while trying to stop the tears. "I'm so sorry. The move has been a lot to handle and I think this has been building up. Please forgive me for being so emotional."

"It's no problem. You can visit the house anytime. Really, I want you to visit," she told me, offering me a box of tissues.

"Thank you. I just need to get some decent sleep and get settled. I'm glad we moved, and I love our new house. But so many memories are here."

When we moved away from our first house in Homewood to live in the Southside neighborhood of the city, we left the only neighborhood we had lived in since my husband and I had married five and a half years before. We left the streets we had walked as newlyweds and the streets we had walked as new parents with our daughter in the jogging stroller. We left our neighbors. We left a particular narrative and future that I had wanted for so long. When I sat in front of the fireplace that had held our Christmas stockings, I grieved more than the loss of our house and my memories. I grieved the loss of my future in this place. It felt like I was losing someone I loved.

Ashley Hales believes our houses can seem human because they "carry our pain, and shelter what is most dear to us." She adds, "Houses are more than mere objects, more than status symbols, more than indicators of class and privilege. We hope, of course, to find home in them. But we also hope to find ourselves." When I moved away from that house in Homewood, I had to let go of not only the home but also the self I had found there.

Memories—ordinary and extraordinary—are hard for me to separate from their birthplaces. The four homes I've lived in as an adult are chalices, of sorts, from whose rims I taste the memories of my marriage, children, friends, and neighbors. I drink in the streets and landscapes that unfurl from front doors; spiritual consolations and desolations; seasons of mental illness and seasons of health; twists and turns along my vocational path; shared meals, celebrations, and conversations; times of heartache, loneliness, and sorrow.

My desire for home, my attachment to places, the entanglement of my memories with the houses in which I've lived: all speak to a deeper truth and a more substantive longing. The idea of heaven as our ultimate home is attractive. I imagine the wholeness I will know in our eternal home, and I try to give my attention to the glimpses of wholeness shining in this life. I experience moments of wholeness when my kids draw close to me to discuss the matters of their souls and when my husband is vulnerable with me about his inner world, his fears, his hopes. When I receive the gift of meaningful interactions with strangers or acquaintances or those to whom I'm closest, I feel less isolated. It's as if we are caught up in the knowledge that we are more of who we were created to be and somehow supernaturally resting comfortably in our eternal home. And in those moments, my physical places are little more than bricks and mortar, and my memories associated with those places seem less significant. But I inhabit more space outside of these moments than within them.

Sometimes I daydream about getting out of Birmingham, out of Alabama. I've lived in this state my entire life, and in this city since I started college, and I can't help but think better places to dwell exist elsewhere. But I don't know if I can ever leave. I don't know if Tim can ever leave. I don't know if we have it in us to move away from our friends and the familiar places that have formed our lives here. I don't know if we have it in us to leave our memories scattered all over the city like crumbs we might need to find our stories and the versions of ourselves that have created who we are now.

During a recent June cold snap, I went to the local botanical gardens for a morning walk. As soon as I passed through the entrance, I was flooded with memories of being there with my children when they were younger. We dedicated many mornings throughout the past sixteen years to walking around the gardens and enjoying their beauty. Exploring the gardens was also a great way to help my kids burn some energy and wear them out so they would have good, long naps after we got home—and so I would have a good, long break from mothering them.

I walked the route we always took—past the rose garden, past the lilies, and into the fern glade. By that point, I was weeping so hard that I had to sit down on one of the memorial benches. I couldn't help remembering the many days there with my kids when they were little. But I didn't know why I was crying. My memories from being at the botanical gardens were happy memories. My kids were doing great—we had no difficult issues to navigate or express sorrow over. I didn't wish they were still little. (Trust me.)

Was I grieving because my daughter and son will be venturing out on their own in the next few years? Was I grieving the loss of a simpler season? Was I overwhelmed by the intensity of the memories this place held for me? It probably doesn't matter why I was crying. By the time I finished walking and weeping, my eyes were red and puffy, and I was dehydrated. I had worn myself out and needed a good, long nap.

Leaving Birmingham would mean leaving memories buried in the grounds at the botanical gardens. It would mean leaving memories at the zoo, the science center, the art museum, and the parks my family played at for hundreds (or thousands?) of hours. It would mean leaving my memories hovering around the homes and communities we have lived in, the various places of importance like Five Points, and the churches at which we have worshipped during the past twenty-six years. Leaving Birmingham would mean leaving all of this. And I don't know if we can do it. I don't know if we can face the sort of loneliness created by losing this place.

$$\left(32\right)$$

Nature's Comfort

Connie Small lived much of her adult life alongside her husband, a lighthouse keeper, at outposts scattered up and down the coast of Maine. Soon after they were married, they lived together in lighthouses from the 1920s until 1948, when they extinguished their final light on an early May morning.

Before she married Elson Small, Connie worried about what her life would be like as the wife of a lighthouse keeper. But she was encouraged by her grandmother, who had been a governess for some lighthouse keepers' children and who told her the beauty, purpose, and mission of the lighthouse keeper life would outweigh any loneliness she might feel. And so Connie grew more settled about her future with Elson—even though it meant giving up her own dreams of going to school to pursue her passions of painting and writing. Once married, Connie adapted to a life of sparse accommodations, few companions, and the almost constant work necessary to maintain a lighthouse and its surrounding land.

But her role as a lighthouse keeper's wife was lonesome. One source of comfort Connie turned to when she suffered from loneliness was the natural world. During an afternoon that Elson was ashore and away from their island, Connie was bored, so she decided to dress up in her Sunday clothes—an embroidered georgette blouse, a straw hat adorned with peacock feathers, and a skirt—and walk down to the rocks on the island's shore. While appreciating the beauty of the island, she noticed a small sea snail crawling back into its shell and thought, "I don't have to be lonely with a world of different creatures to be explored."

Several years later, Connie found herself lonely again while Elson was away. This time they were living in a lighthouse on an island in the middle of the Saint Croix River. She felt jealous of her husband's trips to town, which provided him opportunities to talk to other people. In her isolation, she "turned to the nature and the animals, learning that nothing is sufficient unto itself."

Robert P. Harrison introduced the term *species loneliness* in 1995 in an essay titled "Toward a Philosophy of Nature." In a 2005 podcast episode, he elaborated on what he means by the term:

> [M]any of us today who inhabit urban first-world environments suffer from a malaise for which there is no name. Let's call it, for lack of a better term, "species loneliness." Since our millennial beginnings, human beings have always shared their worlds, their homes, their nights and days, with animals. I don't mean pets, I mean our animal neighbors. Now all of a sudden many of us live in worlds without animals, without the diurnal

and nocturnal presence of animal sounds. Why is this not an issue for us? What are the effects on us of finding ourselves—and feeling ourselves—utterly alone as a species? What happens to our souls when we lose suddenly this ancient kinship with the animal kingdom?

Harrison brings up a point many of us have not considered. If people seem to be lonelier now than in the past, maybe it's due in part to our greater separation from other living beings in the animal kingdom. Maybe Connie's interactions with animals and nature on the islands she inhabited as a lighthouse keeper's wife mitigated her sense of species loneliness. It's possible being closer to nature, its creatures, and their creaturely sounds helped her feel less alone and more connected to the world around her.

I thought about Connie Small as I was reading science journalist Florence Williams's book, *The Nature Fix*. Williams began studying the effects of nature because she believed people were losing their connection to the natural world. That loss, shows Williams, has real deleterious effects: higher stress levels, blood pressure, and anxiety. Conversely, intimacy with nature has all sorts of positive effects. For example, a 2009 Dutch study cited by Williams found that people who live near more vegetation are less lonely than those in similar income brackets who live near less.

A few days after reading Williams on nature, I found myself reading the psalmist on nature:

The heavens are telling the glory of God;
    and the firmament proclaims his handiwork.
Day to day pours forth speech,

and night to night declares knowledge.
There is no speech, nor are there words;
    their voice is not heard;
yet their voice goes out through all the earth,
    and their words to the end of the world.
In the heaven he has set a tent for the sun,
which comes out like a bridegroom from his wedding
    canopy,
    and like a strong man runs its course with joy.
Its rising is from the end of the heavens,
    and its circuit to the end of them;
    and nothing is hid from its heat. (Ps 19:1-6)

In his commentary on this psalm, John Calvin offers insight into our response to God's creation: "When a man, from beholding and contemplating the heavens, has been brought to acknowledge God, he will learn also to reflect upon and to admire his wisdom and power as displayed on the face of the earth, not only in general, but even in the minutest plants." So perhaps even the clover in the cracks of the sidewalk has the capacity to turn my attention to our Creator. To again draw on Calvin: "there is nothing in the ordinary course of nature, throughout the whole frame of heaven and earth, which does not invite us to the contemplation of God."

When vacationing at the coast, I love sitting in a beach chair with my feet in the sand. I watch the waves crash, and my soul awakens as I become more aware of God's glory and beauty. When I'm at a cabin in the mountains, I enjoy the views that proclaim God's majesty. I also feel connected to God and creation throughout the course of my everyday life. When I walk in my neighborhood and feel the sun on my face and notice small creatures such as lizards and birds and butterflies. When I drive on the expressway and catch a great view of a sunset or a rainbow. When I arrive home late on a summer night and remember to look up at the starry sky while cicadas hum and click around me.

I don't live at a lighthouse or in another environment filled with the kinds of opportunities Connie Small had to observe and interact with the natural world. But I can open my eyes and give my attention to the slices of creation around me. I can behold God's glory revealed to me through ways unique to my place—even if it seems less exotic than a beach or the mountains or an island with a lighthouse. And when I see and receive the gifts of nature, I am reminded that I belong to my place, to this world, to our God.

(33)

Drawing What's in Front of Us

I first read Alain De Botton's *The Art of Travel* in 2005. My favorite chapter was "On Possessing Beauty," in which De Botton writes about John Ruskin and his ideas about the value of drawing—how it encourages us to notice details, and how it helps us connect to beauty and place. De Botton writes:

> In explaining his love of drawing (it was rare for him to travel anywhere without sketching something), Ruskin once remarked that it had arisen not from a desire "for reputation, [or] for the good of others, [or] for my own advantage, but from a sort of instinct *like that of eating or drinking*." What unites the three activities is that they all involve assimilations by the self of desirable elements from the world, a transfer of goodness from without to within. As a child, Ruskin said, he had so loved the look of grass that he had frequently wanted to eat it, but

gradually he had discovered that it would be better to try to draw it: "I used to lie down on it and draw the blades as they grew—until every square foot of meadow, or mossy bank, became a *possession* to me."

I still have a drawing of the room I stayed in at a bed-and-breakfast during a solo beach trip in August 2005. On the first night of my four-day vacation away from my husband and our two young children, I put what I had recently learned from De Botton and Ruskin into practice. I sat on the bed, my back against the mahogany headboard, a sketchbook on my lap, and drew what was right in front of me—an armoire, windows, a reading chair, a floor lamp.

It takes little effort to recall memories of my guest room and how I used my time while I was in Rosemary Beach more than fourteen years ago. Days on the beach under an umbrella with a stack of books and magazines. Dinner (twice) at an upscale northern Italian restaurant, where I ate (both times) sautéed scallops nestled atop the most perfect lemon risotto and drank (both times) a few glasses of cold, crisp Prosecco. Dinner on my final night was at a wine bar within walking distance where I drank red wine, shared platters of cheese and charcuterie, and discussed faith and motherhood with an older couple from Texas. A late-afternoon shopping trip when I purchased two half-priced fancy dresses for my daughter and a soft, seafoam green Rosemary Beach T-shirt for my husband. A pink and orange sunset viewed from the edge of the water while a swarm of dragonflies looped and spiraled around me. A breakfast of eggs, sausage, and coffee on the morning of my departure.

I'm not 100 percent sure that drawing the room I stayed in helps me remember the details of my trip or develop a deeper connection to Rosemary Beach. I like to believe giving my attention to my surroundings, in a way that wasn't typical for me, led to a fuller experience of my time there. De Botton and Ruskin would probably encourage me to keep traveling along this line of thinking.

Ruskin didn't think drawing was dependent on talent. Rather, he thought drawing was vital because "it could teach us to see—that is, to notice rather than merely look." As we draw what is in front of us, we gain a more informed understanding of how it is truly formed, and that leads to sharpened memories of it. Ruskin believed drawing was more important than writing and that more emphasis should be placed on drawing instruction. He told a royal commission on drawing in 1857, "My efforts are directed not to making a carpenter an artist, but to making him happier as a carpenter."

I have accumulated other drawings over the years. The Communion table at a former church. The exterior of a friend's beach home. The front porch on our old house in Southside. A jar of paint brushes in a friend's art studio. The view from my favorite spot at my favorite table at my local public library. Right now, I'm thinking about more drawings I can create. I'm thinking about places I encounter daily and other meaningful places I visit less frequently—the places to which I belong.

Part IV

BELONGING THROUGH ART

Poems for the Dead

I do not always understand poems. Some days I have to reread a poem multiple times before I comprehend any meaning. On other days I just let the sound wash over me and worry less about understanding. I keep reading for the linguistic precision, for the sharpness of image, for what a metaphor can sometimes suddenly show me.

Poets see more clearly the spaces that terrify us, and they are more equipped (or perhaps just more willing) to enter those spaces. Anna Kamienska, Audre Lorde, Dionisio D. Martínez, Max Ritvo—they have framed loneliness with nouns and verbs and rhyme and meter. Their poems give us language for the haunting elements of unbelonging that we are unable to put words around on our own. Their poems open us up to truths we would rather turn away from, to truths we wish were false.

Martínez's poem, "Flood: Years of Solitude," is one such example. The words attend me toward eternal verities.

To the one who sets a second place at the table anyway.
To the one at the back of the empty bus.
To the ones who name each piece of stained glass pro-
　　jected on a white wall.
To anyone convinced that a monologue is a conversa-
　　tion with the past.
To the one who loses with the deck he marked.
To those who are destined to inherit the meek.
To us.

When I read this poem, I think about my loneliness, but more so the loneliness of others. And the last two words help me consider a sort of corporate loneliness we all shoulder.

In 2001, Dutch poet Bart FM Droog proposed that poets write poems for the "lonely dead" in the city of Groningen in the Netherlands. He wanted to honor those who die in anonymity, those whose bodies are never claimed by family or friends or acquaintances. This practice is now common in many Dutch cities, as well as in parts of Belgium. The poets try to learn as much as they can about each deceased person and pen a fitting poem. Writer Christine Ro, whose essay introduced me to the Dutch practice, notes:

> The lonely funerals phenomenon is especially moving as the Netherlands is a largely non-religious society: two-thirds of the population has no religious affiliation. Death would be sharpest for those who don't believe in an afterlife, and the non-religious would have little reason to believe that dead souls could somehow be comforted by

the words written to mark their lives. So the significance of this ritual, even more than other funeral practices, is for the living.

The poems—Ro calls them "short, stark, and moving speculations on identity and loss"—help us hold the tragedy of anonymous deaths. I find comfort in knowing these dead people, who were most likely neglected while they were alive, are remembered.

It's no surprise poets have stepped into the gaps that are formed by lonely deaths. Many who are grieving the loss of loved ones turn to poetry for comfort and meaning. After his father died, poet Kevin Young searched for a poetry collection about death to help him navigate his new reality. When he couldn't find what he needed, he decided to create an anthology himself. In an interview with National Public Radio, Young explained why poetry is vital when people we love die. He described how poets and their words help people explore their feelings and find language for the grief associated with death. Poems are able to "capture a moment, a feeling, perhaps a fleeting feeling" for those who are full of sorrow and sadness. "Since I lost you, I am silence-haunted," says one of the poems, written by D. H. Lawrence, in Young's collection. "Sounds wave their little wings / A moment, then in weariness settle / On the flood that soundless swings."

$$\left(35 \right)$$

Music and Memories

Recent measurements of brain activity recorded while people were listening to music depicted an experience most of us have had: being transported back in time by a song. Armed with their imaging, scientists explain that the medial prefrontal cortex, which is located right behind the eyes, collects music, memory, and emotion and braids them together as we listen and respond to songs from long ago. While we listen to old, familiar songs, our past combines with the present and we are in two places at the same time.

Whenever I hear Peter Cetera belt out "Waiting for the break of day" in the song "25 or 6 to 4," I'm carried back to the brick house on Hunting Creek Road in Montgomery, Alabama, where I lived as a child. I'm four years old. I'm on the rust-colored shag carpet and can smell the drywall and new paint in our den that had doubled in size. I see my dad hanging his new Bose 901 speakers and setting up his sound system, including a Philips turntable.

My Barbie dolls are probably not far from my reach. I most likely ate a bowl of Frosted Flakes for breakfast.

That song and others on the album are my earliest music memory. *Chicago IX: Chicago's Greatest Hits* was released on November 10, 1975, when I was seven months old, and it became one of my dad's favorite albums. He played it for years in our home. The lyrics and melodies are embedded in my mind, in my body, in my core. They made a home in me the way small animals burrow into the ground and form a place to dwell.

I was twelve years old when 10,000 Maniacs's *In My Tribe* was released. It was 1987, and this was the first cassette tape I bought with my own money. It was also the first cassette tape I bought with my own brain. I discovered this music without anyone's assistance in the record store, and I preferred to listen to it instead of the typical Top 40 music most of my friends loved. I purchased the CD when it became available, and now I pull it up on Spotify. I still listen to this album, as a married mom of two kids who are just a couple of years older than I was when I discovered Natalie Merchant's music. I sing along to the whole thing—from Merchant's vowel-y vocal run in the intro of "What's the Matter Here?" to her closing *ah la las* of "Verdi Cries."

The songs from *In My Tribe* take me back to my bedroom in middle school and high school, when I'd stay up late on the phone with George or Kellie or Julie, Merchant's voice the soundtrack for our conversations. I'm also in my college dorm room, when the lyrics about politics, justice, life, and love became more meaningful as I discussed big ideas with my classmates and professors. And I'm in the passenger seat of the black Camry my husband drove when we were dating. We're singing along to "Like the Weather" and "Don't Talk" while holding hands and running errands. This album helps me remember people I love and have loved, as well as my past selves that have helped form who I am now.

Throughout my teens and into early adulthood, I viewed Merchant as a sort of long-distance older sister, and her songs were her letters to me. Her words spoke into my adolescent angst and aloneness. For whatever reason—because of them or because or me or because of all of us—I found it difficult to have significant conversations with most of my friends, classmates, and family members. Merchant's music took me into deeper places and fulfilled a desire for more substance absent from many of my relationships.

When I was recovering from a several-months season of major depression in 2008, my taste in music expanded. I listened to a wide range of artists on Pandora, choosing from the smorgasbord of what seemed like unlimited choices. I often gravitated to the Beyoncé station when I needed energy to combat the side effects from my medications. "Crazy in Love," "Single Ladies," "Check On It," and "Irreplaceable" accompanied me while I was working out or when I needed motivation to clean my house and do the mountains of laundry that seem to reproduce like protozoa.

On many of these depressed days, I forced myself to grab my iPhone and earbuds, crank up the music, and go outside. After walking just one block, I was always more alert and had an improved outlook on life. With Beyoncé's lyrics and impressive range as my walking partners, I navigated the twenty-minute loop around my neighborhood, sometimes adding subtle dance moves along the way. Some studies show listening to music can release dopamine in our brains and improve vigor, while reducing depression, tension, and anger. I suppose there are worse ways to self-medicate than listening to R & B.

During my second major manic episode in June 2011, I returned to the familiar Beyoncé station on Pandora. But I wasn't interested in working out or doing laundry. I wasn't using Beyoncé to increase my vigor; I was trying to escape my paranoia and hallucinations. The music replaced my thoughts and gave me something to hang on to. Listening to Beyoncé reminded me I had come out on the other side of a cycle of intense mania and depression before, so I could come out on the other side again. My iPhone and earbuds connected me to comfort and offered me hope. Music lifted me out of the pit. It pulled me into a past version of myself that was still a part of me, a past version of myself that was less alone, less isolated.

On a spring afternoon many years ago, a severe thunderstorm knocked out the power at our house for several hours. Because it was the time of day when darkness was starting to descend, my kids and I gathered and lit several candles and placed them on the coffee table in our family room. We connected an iPhone to a battery-powered speaker and played *The Beatles* (a.k.a. *The White Album)*. My husband, our daughter (who was ten years old at the time), our son (then eight), and I sat on the oatmeal-colored sectional and didn't move for the entire ninety-three minutes and twenty-six seconds while the album played. In the glowing candlelight, we listened and sang along to "Ob-La-Di, Ob-La-Da," "Rocky Raccoon," and "Helter Skelter."

When I listen to the *White Album* now, I remember that night in our family room. We were all present to each other. We weren't distracted by screens. The music we shared served as a binding agent for our family. It created something communal, something lasting.

$$\left(36\right)$$

Portraits of Loneliness

Photographer Paola Zanni created a photograph series of various depictions of loneliness in Japan. Thirty images show individuals and groups of people in different settings, and hints of isolation are evident in the faces, bodies, postures, and landscapes of every framed subject.

A man eats by himself at a restaurant counter. People shuffle down a city block at night under the glow of streetlights and neon signs. A woman is barely visible in a second-floor window. A lone man stands under an umbrella in the rain, staring at his phone. A vast, still sea appears to hold a single boat in the distance.

Writing about photography, photographers, and loneliness, Hanya Yanagihara observes:

The annals of photography contain many extraordinary portraits, but the ones we linger on longest achieve something exceptional: they suggest that in the microsecond it takes for the shutter to blink, some communion has been found, that an unseen life has become a seen one, that attention has been paid, that an act of witness has been accomplished.

Looking closely at Zanni's images from Japan, we as viewers desire to truly *see* those who have been photographed. Feelings of understanding and empathy may rise, move over, and make room for hope, because we see others being seen. The unseen are seen. The lost are found. And if it's possible for others to be seen in their loneliness, maybe we can be seen in ours.

$$\left(37\right)$$

When Stories Help

I settled on the brown leather sofa in the corner of our great room with a copy of Gin Phillips's *Fierce Kingdom* and finished reading it four hours later. I shooed away my mostly self-sufficient children. "Let me read unless you're bleeding or can't breathe."

The story of a mother and her young son trapped at their local zoo during a terrorist attack held my attention. I didn't skim. I didn't skip pages. I grasped onto every word right from the opening sentences, which describe the mother's physical sensations as she stooped down to play with her son. Phillips writes,

> For a long while Joan has managed to balance on the balls of her bare feet, knees bent, skirt skimming the dirt. But now her thighs are giving out, so she puts a hand down and eases onto the sand.
>
> Something jabs at her hip bone. She reaches underneath her leg and fishes out a small plastic spear—no

longer than a finger—and it is no surprise, because she is always finding tiny weapons in unexpected places.

These first two paragraphs on the first page made me trust Phillips, the narrator, and Joan, the mother. It's a simple scene—a mother playing with her child. But the attention to Joan's body here and throughout the rest of the book helped me connect with the story. Mothering is an embodied act. Sometimes we get stuck in our heads because of the decisions we have to make every day, every week, every year. What are we supposed to feed our children? How much sugar is too much? What about their sleep schedules? Where should we live? Which schools? Screen time or no? And how are we supposed to discipline them, correct them, and teach them to be kind? The thinking and overthinking fools us into believing this is what mothering is all about. If we are thinking and making decisions, we are mothering. And we are. But we are whole beings with bodies and souls in addition to minds, and we give our full selves to our children whether or not we notice our offering.

So when I read a book about a mother and her son in which the author gives attention to the mother's body, I remembered my own body. I remembered playing with the plastic dump trucks in the mulch with my kids at Triangle Park a few miles from our house. I remembered feeling the heat of the summer sun during our twice-daily "nature walks" around our neighborhood, picking up fallen limbs to use as walking sticks and smelling the flowers in Mr. Don's yard. I remembered sharing sweet, cold watermelon with my toddler son under an umbrella on the beach with his sweaty, sandy body leaning into my belly and chest. I remembered the hug I gave my daughter a few nights ago before she went to bed—how she squeezed me tight even though she's a teenager and is separating from me more and more every day. I remembered giving birth to both of my children. The pressure and the pain and the glory.

These aren't the sorts of things most mothers discuss over coffee. We usually stick to chitchat about our schedules and work and upcoming vacations and all of the questions and answers that help us make the decisions we need to make as we care for our children. When our conversations go deeper, we may discuss fears and hopes, maybe even sex. But no one has ever asked me how my mothering happens in my body. Two paragraphs of a book about a terrorist attack at a zoo helped me ponder that question.

Joan became a new friend who invited me to approach my role as a mom from a more holistic perspective. When I moved into this new place where my body mattered, I was more connected to myself and the mothers around me who were also embodied beings. I viewed our bodies as more than containers that hold the stuff that matters. Our bodies matter, too.

When I read another book, *The Golden State* by Lydia Kiesling, I had to take the story in slowly because it transported me back to the exhausting mundaneness of parenting little kids. Meeting the needs of young children, who were so very dependent on me for their survival, was tiring. And I was going insane. Maybe it was exhausting because I was going insane. Or maybe I was going insane because it was exhausting. Either way, it was a difficult season.

As I read about Daphne, a young mother, and her daughter, Honey, my heart raced, my hands got clammy, and my concentration waned. I'd read a few pages about the daytime minutiae of a mother caring for her child and the nighttime ritual of the same mother sneaking outside to smoke a cigarette, and then I'd take a break for a day or so. Then I'd read a few more pages before taking another break. After reading the first couple dozen pages, I messaged the author, who is an acquaintance: "I love your book but I have to read it in small doses because it's taking me back to one of the hardest seasons of my life when my kids were little and I was suffering from undiagnosed and untreated mental illness. Your portrayal of motherhood is too good."

Kiesling writes early in the book:

> Finally we sit in the big bed and have milk which is warm in the sippy cup from this morning because I haven't brought a carton and we have two stories *Goodnight Moon* and *Goodnight Gorilla*, trying to emphasize the goodnight aspect and the sleeping aspect, and I decide to forgo brushing teeth and then think no no no it's too easy to fail to establish good habits and I haul her into the bathroom and poke at her with the toothbrush and she clamps her mouth shut and cries and then I lay her in the Pack 'n Play turn on the sound machine say "I love you I love you I love you" and close the door and listen to her scream.

This scene is perfectly portrayed with details I identify with so strongly that I have to wonder if Kiesling has written about my own life—the time we took our young daughter with us to a family wedding in Tampa and she was off her schedule and in a strange place and we did all of the things we normally did at home when getting ready for bed because that's the point of having routines, but it made no difference. Our daughter was grumpy and fussy and unhappy about sleeping in a portable crib we managed to fit inside the closet in our room.

Kiesling's long sentences and missing commas create a sense of alertness. I returned to when my daughter and son were little and I was trying to figure out what they needed and what I needed and the constant mental gymnastics I performed whenever I was trying to figure out what they needed and what I needed.

But after several hours with *The Golden State* over the course of many weeks, I realized Kiesling's writing wasn't only making me feel anxious; her words and scenes were also making me feel seen and known. I wasn't the only mother who worried and agonized over parenting decisions. I wasn't the only mother who was thrilled when her children finally fell asleep. I wasn't the only mother who doubted if she was doing this whole motherhood thing the right way. Focusing on the fact that the book helped me be seen and known allowed me to let go of the anxiety I felt while I read.

The Golden State also reminded me of how valuing the ordinary transformed my mothering. While the details of the mundane were overwhelming at times, they were also comforting. When my daughter was four years old and my son was two, I was diagnosed with bipolar disorder. I had a paradigm shift. I learned to let go of some of my expectations, give my attention to the present moment, and be more available to my kids without feeling the need to control them. I didn't always inhabit this new posture with my children, but when I was able to do so, we all benefited.

I saw Daphne inhabiting a similar posture while she parented her daughter, and it made me wish we were friends. In some sort of alternate universe, the me of twelve years ago is texting with Daphne after our kids are down for their afternoon naps. We are on our front porches, smoking cigarettes, and in between drags we are commiserating over the beauty and horror of motherhood.

$$\left(38 \right)$$

Visio Divina

When I walked into the Georgia O'Keeffe Museum in Santa Fe on a hot August afternoon, the first painting my attention turned toward was O'Keeffe's *Trees in Autumn*. Most of the trees in this work are portrayed with flames of bright red, orange, and gold. A single green fir provides a touch of realism and stands as a stark contrast to the colorful ribbons of leaves on the more surreal deciduous trees. A background of lavender hills and blue sky, along with layers of crawling light, create that familiar feeling of being outside in the hour or so before the sun begins to set.

I was attending a weeklong arts and writing workshop, and participants had gathered at the museum with the workshop's chaplain for *visio divina*. The spiritual practice of *visio divina* is similar to *lectio divina*, when readers take time to interact slowly and deeply with Scripture through meditation and prayer. While *lectio divina* is the practice of divine reading, *visio divina* is the practice of divine *seeing*. As the Upper Room website explains,

"*visio divina* invites one to encounter the divine through images."
Prayerfully beholding a photograph, an icon, a piece of art, or
other visual representation provides an opportunity to experience
God in unique and compelling ways.

I had practiced *visio divina* once before, but on this day in
Santa Fe, I devoted more time to divine seeing. The chaplain had
instructed us to stand before two or three of O'Keeffe's paintings for several minutes and open to what God might have for
us through our engagement with the artist's work as we lingered,
looked, and listened.

After several minutes, I left *Trees in Autumn* and moved through
the gallery until another piece stood out to me. *Autumn Trees–The
Maple* is also a colorful painting, but it's more muted than *Trees in
Autumn*. It has more white space, some gray, a touch of gloom. The
shape and outline of the tree are difficult to discern. It's an idea of a
tree, a tree that is only a tree because the artist said it is.

The painting brought to mind the landscape of late fall,
when winter is near and temperatures are cool. Again, I stood
with the painting for several minutes and tried to interpret my
inner response. I enjoyed the stillness and the process of giving my
attention to the art. O'Keeffe's work invited me to enter a realm
that wasn't affected by the news of the day, my personal anxieties,
or unknown passersby. I entered this dimension and considered
how the painting might see me. Was it a mirror that reflected an
image of my soul? If so, what was it trying to show me? I stood in
front of this painting, asking questions and waiting for answers.
After the energy of my asking and waiting fizzled, I wandered
away to see what else there was to see.

I arrived in a larger gallery and glanced back over my right shoulder. In the corner was a dark painting that I was immediately drawn to. I sat down on the end of a nearby bench and observed this third piece for several minutes. *Black Place III* has shades of gray, black, and white mountainous shapes. A muted yellow crack or narrow stream makes a crooked path down a portion of the middle of the work. Red shadows splash near the bottom. I eventually discovered two eyes in the middle of the painting. Or the suggestion of two eyes. The painting was dark. Very dark. And I loved it.

After I recognized I was more drawn to this piece than I had been to the other two, I began to berate myself. "Of course I prefer the dark painting. Why do I always lean toward the hard, sorrowful, sad things? Why am I like this? Why do I feel most comfortable in the murkiness?" I stayed with these questions and tried to not shy away from the feelings they produced. Then my thoughts were interrupted by this observation: "But you were drawn to colorful paintings, too. You were drawn to colorful paintings first."

Black Place III was a mirror, and it reflected my doubts back to me. Its eyes might have even been looking at me. The painting ignited questions—asked with a tone of judgment and ridicule—about the essence of who I am. I've long been aware of my tendencies to stray toward hard things, to acknowledge and make room for brokenness. But my harsh views about the truth of who I am only surfaced after I practiced *visio divina* in the Georgia O'Keeffe Museum. At first it was uncomfortable to realize I was judging myself, but I was also thankful to see my inner world with greater clarity. Then, when I noticed the interruption and saw *more* of the truth—I was also drawn to color and brightness and lightness—my soul settled. It was as though God were telling me, "You are *all* of who I created you to be."

Part V

BELONGING TO GOD

$$\left(\begin{array}{c} 39 \end{array}\right)$$

Living with Complexities

I had to go through a pile of mail when my family and I returned home from a brief trip to attend my niece's wedding. I picked up the stack and sorted it into the three piles: trash it, handle it, and read it later. Then there's the weekly church newsletter. It doesn't go in a pile because I always read it immediately. It's not a very fancy newsletter. It wouldn't be considered noteworthy by anyone who doesn't go to my church. But *I* go to my church, and the newsletter interests me, so I read it when I see it.

On the front page of every issue of my church's newsletter is a brief note from one of our pastors. I was pleased to see the subject of this note was loneliness. "You have no need to feel lonely," my pastor wrote. "Not only were you created by a God who knew you intimately before you were born, but you were redeemed by his Son who suffered the worst loneliness on your behalf, so you don't have to."

I slowed down and reread his words. Did he really think people who believe in Jesus shouldn't ever struggle with loneliness?

That Jesus's death and resurrection were a once-and-for-all cure for something that I was becoming certain was a part of the human condition? I thought about this pastor's note for days. I felt disappointed, and then enraged, and then a bit more charitable. I concluded two things, that one, my pastor was trying to say something concisely that required more space, and two, we need more words for *loneliness*.

Because loneliness means different things to different people and our experiences of isolation can shift as our circumstances change, it might be useful to expand our language. I recently heard a story on National Public Radio about the language of anger and the benefits of naming specific types of anger. Michaeleen Doucleff explained how several variations of anger exist in the United States "like exuberant anger when you're getting pumped up to compete in sports, or sad anger when your spouse or boss doesn't appreciate you." Other cultures have even more varieties. She said Germans have a word, *backpfeifengesicht*, that basically means "a face in need of a slap." They use this word when they are so enraged that the face of the person they're furious with seems to be urging them to punch it.

When I heard about how naming our different types of anger can help us explore and regulate our emotions, I thought this technique might be transferable to how we discuss and consider our loneliness. Maybe my pastor was referring to the particular strain of loneliness that *is* relieved by knowing we are God's children who have been redeemed. But we experience many forms of isolation and dejection beyond this one variety.

I asked Beth Young, a counselor in Gainesville, Florida, if she has seen Christian clients who struggle with loneliness and are unable to be soothed by God's truths. Young told me about a woman from an affluent town who felt like everyone around her lived on a conveyor belt. "Go to college. Get married. Have kids. Invest wisely. Wear the shoes. Go to the resort. Have the benevolent hobby. Send out the Christmas cards. She craved something Other and couldn't shake it. She carried great loneliness there." This strain of lonelinss lingers when you try so hard to force yourself into a cookie cutter lifestyle and you wonder if you will ever fit.

Young added another example.

Now that I am living next to a very competitive, respected public university, the mask loneliness wears looks like a twenty-year-old workaholic-in-training, fueled by anxiety, and farming out value through internships, resumes, and an insatiable desire for someone to like her even if she feels like a total sham. I literally got in my car and screamed for a solid sixty seconds after hearing a senior tell me about her last two years of college. I'd never done that before. The story is becoming painfully common—the good Christian girl with the perfect grades and the straight shot to the prized position meets with life's gut punches . . . and now she is branded "failure." And while she watches a friend get the job she'd sacrificed so much for, the loneliness screams longer and louder than I ever could.

This strain of loneliness lingers when you strive and strive to earn approval and acceptance that will never satisfy.

If we turn to the Bible, which tells us pretty early on it is not good for a human to be alone, we find plenty of evidence of loneliness. Several of the Psalms offer us language for our loneliness:

> I am forgotten as though I were dead;
>> I have become like broken pottery. (Ps 31:12)

> God gives the desolate a home to live in;
>> he leads out the prisoners to prosperity,
>> but the rebellious live in a parched land.
>> (Ps 68:6)

> I am like an owl of the wilderness,
>> like a little owl of the waste places.
>> I lie awake;
>> I am like a lonely bird on the housetop.
>> (Ps 102:6-7)

God doesn't always remove our feelings of aloneness or circumstances of aloneness, yet God is always present and offers to sustain us in our suffering. Loneliness is complex, however, and sometimes lingers longer than we wish. My pastor was right—Jesus suffered excruciating loneliness on our behalf. We can wait with expectation for the coming day when God will wipe away every tear from our eyes, when there will be no more death or mourning or crying or pain, when the old order of things will have passed away, when we will fully belong to ourselves, to others, and to God.

In the meantime, we live with our various forms of loneliness. We see loneliness as something that comes and goes and sometimes stays. We see it as something that helps us recognize our need for God and people. And regardless of the specific names we give to our different understandings of loneliness, all forms call us toward the same hope. Even if we have unique descriptions for the isolation we experience, we have a common desire for the everlasting goodness, peace, and rest we know is coming.

Young told me how she views hope and loneliness—for herself and for her clients. She said:

> I've come to think of hope as a never-ending record scratch on the most beautiful song we've ever heard . . . and we just want to hear the end. We can imagine what it would be like, but we can't be satisfied until we know for sure. Loneliness kicks in on day one hundred of that record scratch, and it seems like we are the only one who still hears it. Everyone else hears something beautiful and complete, and we are stuck with the same worn-out notes that have lost their appeal with repetition. The sound of them even hurts our ears. I acknowledge the dissonance. And I wait. I don't lie about how fun hope is. And when I am courageous, I say: When the scratching stops and we can hear the whole song, it will be the most beautiful thing we have ever heard. It will be the only song we never tire of hearing.

Absence

Every now and then I remember what a pastor once said to me after I had told him about the spiritual void I was experiencing. No matter how hard I tried to create spiritual intimacy, God seemed too far off, too distant, and my loneliness was swallowing me.

My pastor listened. His eyes didn't shift from mine even though my eyes were heavy with tears. Plenty of potential distractions vied for his attention in the small coffee shop, but he listened attentively to me.

When I finished describing the void, we sat in silence for a minute or so. Then he said, "What if God is most present when it seems like God is most absent?"

$$\left(41\right)$$

Suffering, Resilience, and Our Hope for Shalom

It's the third week of June, and the signs are already noticeable. They are more apparent each morning after I drink my coffee, when I fail to fall into my normal daily rhythm. Early signs of depression are like the rows of letters when an optometrist adjusts the lenses during a vision exam. At first the signs are just the blurred images of shapes that might be an *E* or a *B*, an *R* or a *P*, an *O* or a *C*. Then, sometimes slowly and sometimes with a terrible swiftness, they are sharp, unmistaken. I can read the row of letters without a trace of doubt: I'm entering a period of depression. Again. I'm not shocked, because I get depressed every summer. It has just arrived sooner than I anticipated.

I don't want to go anywhere or do anything. I just want to stay in bed under my weighted blanket, or maybe on the living room sofa under my weighted blanket. I don't have the brain space or concentration to read or write. I don't want to take my kids to the places they want or need to go. Changing out of my pajamas, walking to the car, and getting ready to drive somewhere feels like an insurmountable series of toilsome steps.

I wind up staying on the sofa during the day. I sleep there at night. When I'm lying on the sofa, my direct view includes our dining table, custom-built by an older gentleman in England twelve years ago. It's fashioned from reclaimed wood that came from a torn-down church or barn or home. We used to eat dinner around this table every night, but since my kids have become teenagers, we rarely eat together. Most of our family meals are meals out—brunch after church or burgers on a weeknight after everyone gets home from their various activities becase this is the season we're in right now. We have plenty of quality family time at night and on the weekends, but I wonder if one of the reasons I'm depressed is our lack of regular meals together.

This view also includes two bookshelves—one holds a fraction of my books and one holds the crockery and glassware we couldn't fit into our tiny kitchen's limited storage space. Wine glasses of assorted sizes and styles. Extra cereal bowls and dinner plates. Serving platters, trivets, and placemats. The full shelves are just some of the proof the condo we bought and moved into two years ago is small and sometimes crowded. I wonder if our lack of space is another reason I'm depressed.

I see a large window, too. Shutters cover most of the panes, but sunshine streams through the high transom window. I'm not in the mood for sunshine. I prefer the dark, the shadows. But I can't do anything to prevent the light from entering.

After three days, I begin to do what I know I'm supposed to do. I make a list of every commitment and task I've been putting off and determine what I can graciously say no to. I email people who are waiting on a response from me, apologize for the delay, and tell them I'm not feeling well and will be in touch soon. I consider how I might be able to increase my margins. I let my clients know I can't take on any new projects for a few months. I hope they will understand.

I do more of what makes me feel better. A spray of my favorite perfume. A walk around my neighborhood. Fresh vegetables—whole pods of okra, sautéed in extra virgin olive oil, sound good. I rinse the okra, throw it in a large iron skillet, and wait. After the color turns the perfect mix of green and brown and gold, I pile the cooked vegetables into a bowl, douse them with sea salt, and eat in silence in the corner of the sofa.

I practice gratitude. For the safe birth of a friend's grandchild. For my husband and our children and the grace they offer me. For our small, cozy condo. For my daughter's final orthodontic appointment. For a sudden rainstorm. For my favorite novels and memoirs and poems.

I pray. I pray for those whose circumstances are difficult and seem insurmountable. I pray for friends who will soon marry. I pray for friends who are trying to be brave. I pray for people who are grieving. I pray for myself—that God will carry me and keep me close.

I lament. I tell God, "This is hard. This appears to be more than I can handle."

I don't think about everything all at once. I can't. I do one more thing I'm supposed to do. And then another. In the spaces in between, I dig around my soul because I want to discover where my hope might be hiding. I want to find it and hold onto it.

One morning the following week, I drink my coffee. I read the Daily Office from the Book of Common Prayer. I begin writing a new essay. My kids wake and come downstairs, and I suddenly realize I don't have to pretend to be the the mom I want to be; I'm already her. When I discover I've fallen back into my normal routine, I know my depression has lifted. I'm not shocked, because it always goes away after it comes. It just disappeared sooner than I anticipated.

• • •

While connections exist between mental illness and loneliness, loneliness is not a form of mental illness. One can be well and lonely. One can be unwell and not lonely. But my mental illness has taught me how to engage and respond to my loneliness. Actually, my experiences with mania and depression associated with bipolar disorder have helped me engage and respond to all manner of suffering. I don't respond to suffering perfectly, of course, but I'm more curious now. I think about what God might be up to in in the midst of discomfort and pain. I grieve the loss of shalom—the distinct peace that includes not only being in right relationships with self, God, other people, and the world, but also includes *enjoyment* in one's relationships with self, God, other people, and the world. But in this ache,

I want to hope. I want to believe flourishing is possible and shalom will arrive.

Theologian Kelly M. Kapic writes about connections between suffering, shalom, and hope: "When we express our longing for lasting shalom but also confess its current transitory nature, a compelling story develops, one that makes sense of love and yearning without doing violence to the complexity of the current human condition. Rejecting both utopianism on the one hand and despair on the other leads us to what might be called defiant hope."

My bouts of mental illness, and the resilience I've developed over the years, have invited me to dwell in places similar to the one Kapic describes. When I'm lonely or know other forms of suffering, I am slowly becoming more comfortable with my desire for change instead of quoting Bible verses at myself. I no longer tell myself I need to "be content" and "consider it pure joy." I accept my humanity instead of dismissing the existence of my flesh or my will. I admit there's no such thing as a perfect world on this side of heaven instead of being surprised whenever I find more proof of sin or brokenness. But I also refuse to believe God has left me or forsaken me. And all of this leads me to hope—or, when hope is especially difficult, to *hope* for hope.

I return to Kapic, who interprets the shift when we move from despair to hope. He writes, "the wounded saint is not belittled . . . but rather reminded of our Redeemer's . . . concern that still mysteriously moves in and through his compromised creation that so longs for shalom."

I want to know this shift. I want to be transformed by it. When my depression or mania or loneliness returns—like an unwelcome guest I try to avoid by turning out the lights and hiding in the back bedroom—I want to remember I'm wounded but not belittled. I want to watch for the coming shalom when all will be well, when relationships will be right, when enjoyment will abound.

$$\left(42\right)$$

Can Loneliness Be a Good Thing?

While most of the loneliness news from the past few years reports how bad it is for our health, some people have suggested loneliness can be beneficial. Therapist Karyn Hall has argued, "Just as physical pain protects people from physical dangers, loneliness may serve as a social pain to protect people from the dangers of being isolated. It may serve as a prompt to change behavior, to pay more attention to relationships which are needed for survival." And my friend and former therapist, Gordon Bals, recently said this about loneliness: "I do think there is profound good in loneliness. It helps us reflect, make changes, seek more, and make space for God."

I have been fascinated by his statement since I first heard it. He's not speaking from a human survival standpoint. He's saying loneliness can help us grow spiritually. How can loneliness be generative? How can it help us reflect, make changes, seek more, and make space for God?

When I began to give attention to loneliness, I did what I usually do when I process any complicated question: I wrote about it and read about it and talked about it. All the thinking, writing, reading, and talking have removed some of the power loneliness has had over me since I was a young child. My loneliness seems less oppressive, less consuming. It accompanies me for a few hours or a few days or a few weeks, instead of hiding in the shadows of my soul like a monster I don't want to acknowledge.

Now my loneliness reminds me of the striking red-headed woodpecker, with its bright crimson head, black back, and white wing patches, which perched in the trees dotted around our former house. I never knew when the woodpecker would appear, but when it did show up, I noticed it. I watched it. I listened to it. I followed its path. (I realize more than one woodpecker may have appeared throughout the ten years we lived in that house. Please humor me and let me live my single-bird dream.)

My reflections on loneliness have also led to more reflections on God, suffering, and hope. I've moved deeper into theological explorations and discussions with others who know a lot more about all of these topics than I will ever know. I've journaled and prayed and sat with God in the silence that comes with mystery.

So as I reflect on my loneliness in conversations with others and God, I feel less alone. I'm not the only person who wants to understand hard things. We all want to know what God is doing. And while I don't have the answers I want, I do have the God I need.

Reflecting on loneliness and belonging has also led to more thoughtfulness in how I relate to my friends and family in everyday life. I am more intentional about the conversations I have during coffee dates with friends, when I'm hanging out with my husband and my kids, and while I'm with our small group on Sunday nights. I've always appreciated Christian community and meaningful conversations, but somehow this greater awareness of my loneliness has led me to desire greater depth with others. I have more courage to ask about hidden things crawling around the shadowy places. I have more confidence to speak words of peace, hope, and encouragement to others. I have more gumption to demand my teenage kids sit still and listen to me read a poem or a short story or an essay to them at night before bed, because I know stories and poems and essays help us belong.

I'm not saying my loneliness is all better now. I'm not saying it doesn't bother me anymore. But it is different. It's more approachable. It sometimes seems like a guide.

$$\textbf{43}$$

Receiving Grace

Last night I had a terrible nightmare. It was one of those confusing dreams inside of another dream. It was dramatic, involving a baby with meningitis at a college football game. Toward the end of the saga, I was exposed as being insane. Again. My grasp on reality was loose. My memory was unclear. I had put others in danger, had lied to my best friend, and was on the verge of losing her. At one point in the dream, when I didn't remember being at the football game, I said, "I thought it was a dream!" and everyone looked at me like I had been found out.

Dreams are the best, right? Even after I woke and knew the dream wasn't real, a rush of familiar loneliness returned. I felt it pressing down on me as I lay in bed trying to shake off the terror of the night. What do I do when this loneliness shows up?

I try to remember I'm a recipient of the grace of loneliness and the grace of belonging. The grace of loneliness comes in many forms. There's grace to be lonely, to know it's normal to be lonely.

I'm not any less of a person or Christian when I'm lonely, and I'm not any more of a person or Christian when I'm *not* lonely. I don't have to work myself into a tizzy trying to figure out the best way to not be lonely anymore. When loneliness shows up, like a scruffy neighborhood cat begging for attention, I can give it a bowl of milk and be curious. Where might it have come from? What feeds its hunger? What does it ask of me right now?

God will give me grace for my future mania and depression. I may get sick again. I will probably get sick again. When mania or depression returns, I will suffer and experience deep loneliness, but I will also receive what I need hour by hour, day by day. Again and again.

There's grace in knowing my friendships will change. Some will grow and some will end. Some will be stronger than others. New ones will form. I receive God's grace to not need others to fill the hole that loneliness digs. But I also receive God's grace of belonging when people come alongside me and shovel a few piles of dirt into the hole loneliness has dug, emptying it of some of its emptiness.

When my children leave our home, I will experience a sort of loneliness I have never known. I will be ready to enjoy my empty nest, but I will also grieve. I will weep. I will receive the grace I need for the season of sorrow and the new-to-me form of loneliness with its own unique flavor.

I ask God for the grace to remember my former church and its people with fondness and love despite broken dreams, broken hopes, and broken relationships. And I ask God for the grace that allows me to be in my current church and love its people. I accept this grace with hope.

We receive the grace to know the suffering of loneliness will one day end. We are on this side of the already-but-not-yet reality of God's kingdom, still suffering from the effects of sin and brokenness and pain. But the knowledge of what's on the other side gives us hope. What's true *today* also gives us hope because the gospel is real right now, at this moment.

The good news, which is held together by the grace of God, is poured out on us every day, all day. This grace is sufficient for us always, in our weakness and isolation, and in our courage and connectedness. This grace supports us as we explore the waters of loneliness, sustains us as we turn toward hope, and surrounds us as we remain in the Great Belonging.

Questions for Reflection and Discussion

For each chapter or section, consider the following questions from a posture of curiosity:

1. How does this chapter or section help you notice your desires to belong and your experiences of loneliness?
2. What questions does this chapter or section raise for you?
3. How does this chapter or section help you better understand your relationships with yourself, others, and God?
4. In what ways do you agree or disagree with the themes of this chapter or section?
5. What ideas or practices do you want to explore further after reading and pondering this chapter or section?
6. What additional thoughts do you have about this chapter or section?

Meditations for Belonging

Author's Note: I have included these meditations for individuals or groups of people, to be read alone or with others. You can read them as you read the book, and you can also return to them when you might need encouragement while exploring your loneliness and belonging. I hope you take your time and create space to sit with your loneliness and your belonging while considering what God might have for you. May God meet you as you sorrow, remember, receive, celebrate, and hope.

A Meditation for Sitting in Solitude

No believer traverses all the road to heaven in company. There must be lonely spots here and there, though the greater part of our heavenward pilgrimage is made cheerful by the society of fellow travelers. Yet somewhere or other on the road, every Christian will find narrow paths and close places where pilgrims must march in single file.

—*Charles Spurgeon, "Christ's Loneliness and Ours," a sermon published on August 8, 1907*

A Prayer by Saint Ignatius of Loyola

Take, Lord, and receive all my liberty,
my memory, my understanding,
and my entire will,
All I have and call my own.
You have given all to me.
To you, Lord, I return it.
Everything is yours; do with it what you will.
Give me only your love and your grace,
that is enough for me.

Matthew 11:28-30

Come to me, all you that are weary and are carrying heavy burdens, and I will give you rest. Take my yoke upon you, and learn from me; for I am gentle and humble in heart, and you will find rest for your souls. For my yoke is easy, and my burden is light.

It Is Well with My Soul

When peace, like a river, attendeth my way,
When sorrows like sea billows roll;
Whatever my lot, Thou hast taught me to say,
It is well, it is well with my soul.
Though Satan should buffet, though trials should come,
Let this blessed assurance control,
That Christ has regarded my helpless estate,
And hath shed His own blood for my soul.
He lives—oh the bliss of this glorious thought!

My sin, not in part but the whole,
Is nailed to the cross, and I bear it no more,
Praise the Lord, praise the Lord, O my soul!
And Lord haste the day when our faith shall be sight,
The clouds be rolled back as a scroll;
The trump shall resound and the Lord shall descend,
Even so, it is well with my soul.
—*Horatio Spafford*

Psalm 62:5-8

For God alone my soul waits in silence,
    for my hope is from him.
He alone is my rock and my salvation,
    my fortress; I shall not be shaken.
On God rests my deliverance and my honor;
    my mighty rock, my refuge is in God.
Trust in him at all times, O people;
     pour out your heart before him;
     God is a refuge for us. *Selah*

A Prayer for Quiet Confidence, Rite One

O God of peace, who hast taught us that in returning and rest we shall be saved, in quietness and in confidence shall be our strength: By the might of thy Spirit lift us, we pray thee, to thy presence, where we may be still and know that thou art God; through Jesus Christ our Lord. *Amen.*
—*Book of Common Prayer*

A Meditation for Meeting a Friend for Coffee

A few women in the community reached out to me. They recognized me as a frightened lush. I told them about my most vile behavior, and they said, "Me too!" I told them about my crimes against the innocent, especially me. They said, "Ditto. Yay. Welcome." I couldn't seem to get them to reject me. It was a nightmare and then my salvation.

It turns out that welcome is solidarity. We're glad you're here, and we're with you. This whole project called you being alive, you finding joy? Well, we're in on that.

—*Anne Lamott,* Small Victories: Spotting Improbable Moments of Grace

Colossians 3:12-15

As God's chosen ones, holy and beloved, clothe yourselves with compassion, kindness, humility, meekness, and patience. Bear with one another and, if anyone has a complaint against another, forgive each other; just as the Lord has forgiven you, so you also must forgive. Above all, clothe yourselves with love, which binds everything together in perfect harmony. And let the peace of Christ rule in your hearts, to which indeed you were called in the one body. And be thankful. Let the word of Christ dwell in you richly; teach and admonish one another in all wisdom; and with gratitude in your hearts sing psalms, hymns, and spiritual songs to God. And whatever you do, in word or deed, do everything in the name of the Lord Jesus, giving thanks to God the Father through him.

A Prayer Attributed to St. Francis, Rite Two

Lord, make us instruments of your peace. Where there is hatred, let us sow love; where there is injury, pardon; where there is discord, union; where there is doubt, faith; where there is despair, hope; where there is darkness, light; where there is sadness, joy. Grant that we may not so much seek to be consoled as to console; to be understood as to understand; to be loved as to love. For it is in giving that we receive; it is in pardoning that we are pardoned; and it is in dying that we are born to eternal life. *Amen.*
—*Book of Common Prayer*

A Meditation for Taking a Walk Outside

The real and proper question is: why is it beautiful?
—*Annie Dillard,* Pilgrim at Tinker Creek

I was between six and seven when I saw the sea for the first time. I could not turn away my eyes: its majesty, the roaring of the waves, the whole vast spectacle impressed me deeply and spoke to my soul of God's power and greatness.
—*St. Thérèse of Lisieux*

A Prayer for Joy in God's Creation, Rite One

O heavenly Father, who hast filled the world with beauty: Open our eyes to behold thy gracious hand in all thy works; that, rejoicing in thy whole creation, we may learn to serve thee with gladness; for the sake of him through all things were made, thy Son Jesus Christ our Lord. *Amen.*
—*Book of Common Prayer*

Isaiah 40:25-26

To whom then will you compare me,
    or who is my equal? says the Holy One.
    Lift up your eyes on high and see:
    Who created these?
He who brings out their host and numbers them,
    calling them all by name;
because he is great in strength,
    mighty in power,
    not one is missing.

All Creatures of Our God and King

All creatures of our God and King,
Lift up your voice and with us sing,
Alleluia! Alleluia!
Thou burning sun with golden beam,
Thou silver moon with softer gleam!
Thou rushing wind that art so strong,
Ye clouds that sail in heav'n along,
O praise Him! Alleluia!
Thou rising moon, in praise rejoice,
Ye lights of evening, find a voice!
Thou flowing water, pure and clear,
Make music for thy Lord to hear,
O praise Him! Alleluia!
Thou fire so masterful and bright,
That givest man both warmth and light.

And all ye men of tender heart,
Forgiving others, take your part,
O praise Him! Alleluia!
Ye who long pain and sorrow bear,
Praise God and on Him cast your care!
Let all things their Creator bless,
And worship Him in humbleness,
O praise Him! Alleluia!
Praise, praise the Father, praise the Son,
And praise the Spirit, Three in One!
—*St. Francis of Assisi, translated by William H. Draper*

Some Words on Creation

When God created the creation, God made something where before there had been nothing, and as the author of the book of Job puts it, "the morning stars sang together, and all the sons of God shouted for joy" (38:7) at the sheer and shimmering novelty of the thing. "New every morning is the love / Our wakening and uprising prove" says the hymn. Using the same old materials of earth, air, fire, and water, every twenty-four hours God creates something new out of them. If you think you're seeing the same show all over again seven times a week, you're crazy. Every morning you wake up to something that in all eternity never was before and never will be again. And the you that wakes up was never the same before and will never be the same again either.

—*Frederick Buechner,* Wishful Thinking

A Meditation for Going to a Museum

Yet my conviction is that art goes beyond luxury. Art and beauty address the human need for hope. For me, hope is functionally inseparable from beauty, for beauty is a reminder that there is, in the words of Abraham Heschel, "meaning beyond absurdity."
—*Megan Mitchell, "Seeking God's Splendor: Thoughts on Art and Faith"*

Prayers at a Museum

Christians can recognize even the most seemingly profane of contemporary art as a kind of prayer, a venture on the possibility that someone, and Someone, will visit, observe, and respond with grace. But to hear this prayer, Christians need to recognize their own vulnerability and fragility rather than expecting art to affirm our piety and power.

Even Paul seemed to have taken time to visit the artistic works of Athens, observing there a monument dedicated to an unknown god. Far from denigrating the Greeks for their blindness, he commended them for their search, offering to name the God they sought. The landscape of modern and contemporary art is littered with altars to unknown gods. These paintings, sculptures, and installations create an opportunity for Christians to creatively and lovingly name the one in whom all things are made—for "he is not far from any one of us" (Acts 17:27).

—*Daniel A. Siedell, "Prayers at the Museum of Modern Art,"* Christianity Today, *January-February 2015*

Colossians 1:16-17

for in him all things in heaven and on earth were created, things visible and invisible, whether thrones or dominions or rulers or powers—all things have been created through him and for him. He himself is before all things, and in him all things hold together.

Some Words on Seeing Art

Go to a museum and look at no more than two or three works . . . Walk backwards and forwards between them. Go and have a cup of coffee. Come back again. Wander around the museum. Come back again . . . Eventually you will find they open up like one of those Japanese paper flowers in water.
—*Sister Wendy Beckett,* in an interview by David Willock for PBS in late 2000

Some Words on Seeing Possibilities

So, after seeing my work, my desire is that you open the eyes of your heart, and see the world and the people around you a little differently. Instead of being filled with anxiety about the world, we can truly see the prismatic possibilities of the world around us.
—*Makoto Fujimura, "How to 'See' My Painting"*

A Prayer for Going to a Museum

Lord, open my eyes to notice the colors, lines, shapes, textures, skill. Open my soul to your wonder, beauty, vastness, glory, and mystery. May I see the works of art with clarity, and may they see me.

A Meditation toward Hope

Authentic worship means being present to the living God who penetrates the whole of human life. The proclamation of God's word and our response to God's Spirit touches everything that is involved in being human: mind and body, thinking and feeling, work and family, friends and government, buildings and flowers.
—*Eugene Peterson,* The Jesus Way

Therefore, the grace of God is expressed in a relationship of belonging.
—*Richard Keith, writing in light of Karl Barth's theology*

An Opening Prayer

Lord, I feel alone. No person fully knows me. No person perfectly loves me. Draw me near to you. May I be in communion with you and hold on to the truth that I am known and loved by you. Help me know I belong to you.

Psalm 44:23-26

Rouse yourself! Why do you sleep, O Lord?
    Awake, do not cast us off forever!
Why do you hide your face?
    Why do you forget our affliction and oppression?
For we sink down to the dust;
    our bodies cling to the ground.
Rise up, come to our help.
    Redeem us for the sake of your steadfast love.

A Prayer for a Person in Trouble or Bereavement, Rite One

O merciful Father, who hast taught us in thy holy Word that thou dost not willingly afflict or grieve the children of men: Look with pity upon the sorrows of thy servant for whom our prayers are offered. Remember him, O Lord, in mercy, nourish his soul with patience, comfort him with a sense of thy goodness, lift up thy countenance upon him, and give him peace; through Jesus Christ our Lord. *Amen.*

—*Book of Common Prayer*

Romans 8:31-39

What, then, shall we say in response to these things? If God is for us, who can be against us? He who did not spare his own Son, but gave him up for us all—how will he not also, along with him, graciously give us all things? Who will bring any charge against those whom God has chosen? It is God who justifies. Who then is the one who condemns? No one. Christ Jesus who died—more than that, who was raised to life—is at the right hand of God and is also interceding for us. Who shall separate us from the love of Christ? Shall trouble or hardship or persecution or famine or nakedness or danger or sword? As it is written: "For your sake we face death all day long; we are considered as sheep to be slaughtered." No, in all these things we are more than conquerors through him who loved us. For I am convinced that neither death nor life, neither angels nor demons, neither the present nor the future, nor any powers, neither height nor depth, nor anything else in all creation, will be able to separate us from the love of God that is in Christ Jesus our Lord.

Psalm 91

You who live in the shelter of the Most High,
     who abide in the shadow of the Almighty,
will say to the Lord, "My refuge and my fortress;
     my God, in whom I trust."
For he will deliver you from the snare of the fowler
     and from the deadly pestilence;
he will cover you with his pinions,
     and under his wings you will find refuge;
     his faithfulness is a shield and buckler.
You will not fear the terror of the night,
     or the arrow that flies by day,
or the pestilence that stalks in darkness,
     or the destruction that wastes at noonday.
A thousand may fall at your side,
     ten thousand at your right hand,
     but it will not come near you.
You will only look with your eyes
     and see the punishment of the wicked.
Because you have made the Lord your refuge,
     the Most High your dwelling place,
no evil shall befall you,
     no scourge come near your tent.
For he will command his angels concerning you
     to guard you in all your ways.
On their hands they will bear you up,
     so that you will not dash your foot against a stone.

You will tread on the lion and the adder,
    the young lion and the serpent you will trample under foot.
Those who love me, I will deliver;
    I will protect those who know my name.
When they call to me, I will answer them;
    I will be with them in trouble,
    I will rescue them and honor them.
With long life I will satisfy them,
    and show them my salvation.

Thoughts on Hope

Hope about the future (the kind of hope the lonely person is bound to forget) brings true joy in the present, because the gospel preaches to the present trials that they aren't and won't be the final state of affairs. In this way, the gospel brings consolation and comfort to the conscience. So, the lonely person, with the psalmist, cries, "But now, Lord, what do I look for? My hope is in you."
—*Zac Hicks*

A Dream of Heaven

And the King says, "Look! God and his children are together again. No more running away. Or hiding. No more crying or being lonely or afraid. No more being sick or dying. Because all those things are gone. Yes, they're gone forever. Everything sad has come untrue. And see—I have wiped away every tear from every eye!"
—*The Jesus Storybook Bible*

A Closing Prayer

Lord, may I receive comfort from you and your Word. May I have hope for my future because of the real and present and true gospel of grace. I turn to you now in my affliction and receive assurance of your love. My hope is in you. Come, Lord Jesus. Amen.

Acknowledgments

I am grateful to the entire Broadleaf Books team, especially Lil Copan, whose initial guidance was essential as I began writing the manuscript, and Valerie Weaver-Zercher, whose expertise and enthusiasm made this book more of what it was meant to be.

Lauren Winner—my teacher, mentor, and friend—provided valuable insight, suggestions, and encouragement. She is a gift to me. She is a gift to many.

Several people read manuscript drafts or chapters and offered helpful feedback. Thanks especially to David McGlynn, Haley Byrd Wilt, Marjean Brooks, Nancy Carroll, Linda Barrett, Sue Tolle, Sarah Hudspeth, Sarah Orner, Bruce and Kelly Denson, Bradley and Sarah Pinkerton, Zac and Abby Hicks, and Fred and Carrie Teardo. I am also thankful for the prayers and cheers I received from Charlotte Boyd Woodham, Susan Skillen, Gordon Bals, Emily Starke, Gina Hurry, Josh Retterer, Scott Jones, Carla Jean Whitley, Sarah Gates, Candice Ashburn, Elisa Muñoz-Miller, Anna Nash, Margariette Hoomes, Scott and Deborah Hill, and James and Rebecca Henderson.

Many thanks to Beth Young for her insight into loneliness and the Christian faith, and to Jennifer Ditlevson Haglund for helping me think through the idea of *la petite mort*.

David Zahl and CJ Green welcomed my first essays on loneliness at *Mockingbird*. Thank you both for making room for me and my work.

The Collegeville Institute and the Episcopal Diocese of Western North Carolina gave me time and space to write and participate in workshops while I was working on my book proposal and the book's first few chapters. Thank you to my brilliant Collegeville cohort for their gracious advice and recommendations.

The writing life can be a solitary life, but I have been placed in communities full of people who care about the intersection of art and faith and make my loneliness less lonely. I am blessed in many ways by dear friends from Seattle Pacific University's MFA in creative writing program, *Image* journal's Glen Workshop, and the Redbud Writers Guild.

Thank you to my family, who is so supportive of me and my writing. My parents, Bill and Cathy Byrd, have prayed faithfully for me and provided much assistance to help me accomplish my goals. My husband's parents, Richard and Barbara Donlon, have done the same ever since I joined the Donlon clan. My daughter, Riley, inspires me and makes me want to be a better writer. And my son, Brady, teaches me so much about courage and determination.

Finally, thank you, Tim, for the love and grace you offer me every single day. I am so glad we belong to each other.

Notes

Chapter 1

Page 3   "We don't have a word": Marina Keegan, "The Opposite of Loneliness," *Yale Daily News*, May 27, 2012, https://tinyurl.com/ydzdo3pr.

Chapter 2

Page 7   "This kind of loneliness": Tom Varney, *Loneliness* (Colorado Springs: NavPress, 1992), 18.

Chapter 3

Page 11   "People didn't think badly": Richard Berks, "We Need to Get Better at Sharing Our Experiences of Loneliness," MQ: Transforming Mental Health, January 29, 2019, https://tinyurl.com/rsua77h.

Page 12   "The more you try to pretend": Emily White, *Lonely* (New York: HarperCollins e-books, 2010), Kindle edition, 252.

Chapter 7

Page 22   "integrate the prayer of the Psalms": U.S. Catholic Church, *Catechism of the Catholic Church* (New York: Crown Publishing Group, 1995), Kindle edition, 333.

Chapter 9

Page 29   "When it comes to both pet owners": "New Market Research Shows Pets Make Us Feel Less Lonely," Human Animal Bond Research Institute, May 7, 2019, https://tinyurl.com/tabwffe.

Page 29   And *Time* magazine reported on a recent poll: Jamie Ducharme, "Growing Old Is Better With a Pet. Here's Why," *Time*, April 3, 2019, https://tinyurl.com /ur4qgvo.

Chapter 11

Page 35   "Even though the word": Anne-Sophie Brändlin, "Mutterseelenallein," DW.com, March 28, 2014, https://tinyurl.com/thbow2b.

Page 36   "eliminate the possibility of trying": Oliver Loo, *1810 Grimm Manuscripts* (1810 Childrens and Household Tales Kinder und Hausmärchen) (self-pub., 2015), Kindle, 26, 473, 579.

Page 37   "Everyone guesses—I feel this—the degree": This, and ensuing quotes from Barthes' work, come from: Roland Barthes, *Mourning Diary* (New York: Hill and Wang, 2010), 44, 61, 86, 218.

Chapter 12

Page 40 "I used to say to Ruth": Lauren F. Winner, *Still: Notes on a Mid-Faith Crisis* (San Francisco: HarperOne, 2012), 58.

Chapter 13

Page 42 "Loneliness and coldness seem to go side by side": Chen-Bo Zhong and Geoffrey J. Leonardelli, "Cold and Lonely: Does Social Exclusion Literally Feel Cold?" *Psychological Science* 19, no. 9 (September 1, 2008): 838–42.

Chapter 14

Page 45 "Our bodies' abilities to see, smell, hear, taste, and touch": Rebecca Rago, "Emotion and Our Senses," Emotion, Brain, and Behavior Laboratory, October 9, 2014, https://tinyurl.com/uy5j92s.

Chapter 15

Page 49 "According to a survey by researchers": Gretchen Spreitzer, Peter Bacevice, and Lyndon Garrett, "Why People Thrive in Coworking Spaces," *Harvard Business Review,* September 2015, https://tinyurl.com/o9hklor.

Chapter 17

Page 57 "If you live with a writer": Julius Lester, "A Convert's Story," *A God in the House: Poets Talk About Faith,*

Tupelo Press Lineage Series (North Adams, MA: Tupelo Press, 2012), Kindle edition.

Chapter 19

Page 61   "A 2016 study found the tendency": Heather Buschman, "Do These Genes Make Me Lonely? Study Finds Loneliness Is a Heritable Trait," UC San Diego Health, September 20, 2016, https://tinyurl.com/utdh29q.

Chapter 22

Page 73   "It's to make sure you always have someone": Nick Oliver, "Portsmouth Elementary Students Hope to Curb Loneliness with New 'Buddy Bench,'" WSAZ, April 24, 2019, https://tinyurl.com/vyvhvd2.

Page 74   "The 'Happy to chat' bench": Cathy Free, "This Town's Solution to Loneliness? The 'Chat Bench,'" *Washington Post*, July 17, 2019, https://tinyurl.com/qman5og.

Chapter 26

Page 87   "I may not quite know what is going on": Rowan Williams, *Being Christian: Baptism, Bible, Eucharist, Prayer* (Grand Rapids: Eerdmans, 2014), 81.

Chapter 27

Page 90   "The voyage on one level": VocalEssense, "The Voyage with Librettist Charles Bennett," YouTube video, 2:09, September 16, 2016, https://tinyurl.com/rthaccj.

Page 90   "Have you ever known anyone": Andy Steiner, "New Choral Work Combats Elderly Loneliness with Community," MinnPost, October 5, 2016, https://tinyurl.com/t37me3g.

Page 91   "older adults who sang in [a] community choir": Scott Maier, "Community choirs reduce loneliness and increase interest in life for older adults," ScienceDaily, November 9, 2018, https://tinyurl.com/yczgjpan.

Page 92   "So often our experience here and now": Kevin Twit, "Psalm 130 (From the Depths of Woe) – IG6 Version," Indelible Grace Hymnbook, March 2013, https://tinyurl.com/t2xer2k.

Chapter 28

Page 96   "Almighty God, who hast knit together": Book of Common Prayer (New York: Seabury Press, 1979), 194.

Page 96   "Who are these like stars appearing": Theobald Heinrich Schenck, "Who Are These Like Stars Appearing," *The Hymnal 1982: According to the Use of the Episcopal Church* (New York: Church Hymnal Corp, 1985), no. 286.

Page 96   "The Episcopal Hymnal": Scot McKnight, "Interview
             with Fleming Rutledge," *Jesus Creed* (blog), *Patheos,*
             February 10, 2018, https://tinyurl.com/r9z5yzg.

Chapter 31

Page 113   "carry our pain, and shelter what is most dear:" Ashley
             Hales, *Finding Holy in the Suburbs: Living Faithfully
             in the Land of Too Much* (Downers Grove, IL: Inter-
             Varsity Press), Kindle edition, 35.

Chapter 32

Page 118   "I don't have to be lonely with a world": Connie Sco-
             ville Small, *The Lighthouse Keeper's Wife* (Orono: The
             University of Maine Press, 1999), 67, 124.

Page 118   Robert P. Harrison introduced the term: Robert P.
             Harrison, "Toward a Philosophy of Nature," *Uncom-
             mon Ground: Rethinking the Human Place in Nature,*
             ed. William Cronon (New York: W. W. Norton &
             Company, 1995), Kindle edition.

Page 118   "[M]any of us today": Robert P. Harrison, "Andrea
             Nightingale on Epicurus and Epicureanism," *Entitled
             Opinions with Robert Harrison,* November 8, 2005,
             https://tinyurl.com/wrybj7t.

Page 119   Williams began studying the effects of nature: Flor-
             ence Williams, *The Nature Fix: Why Nature Makes
             Us Happier, Healthier, and More Creative* (New York:
             W. W. Norton & Company, 2017), 5, 110.

Page 120 "When a man, from beholding and contemplating": John Calvin, *Commentary on the Book of Psalms* (Complete) (With Active Table of Contents), 2011, Kindle edition.

Chapter 33

Page 122 "In explaining his love of drawing": Emphasis added by De Botton. Alain De Botton, *The Art of Travel* (New York: Pantheon, 2002), 216, 217, 219, 220.

Chapter 34

Page 128 "To the one who sets a second place at the table anyway": Dionisio D. Martínez, "Flood: Years of Solitude," in *Bad Alchemy* (New York: W. W. Norton, 1995).

Page 128 "The lonely funerals phenomenon": Christine Ro, "The Dutch City Poets Who Memorialize the Dead," *Ploughshares,* December 24, 2016, https://tinyurl .com/vs55zcr.

Page 129 "Since I lost you, I am silence-haunted": D. H. Lawrence, "Silence," in *The Art of Losing: Poems of Grief and Healing,* ed. Kevin Young (London: Bloomsbury Publishing), Kindle edition, 15.

Chapter 35

Page 130 "Recent measurements of brain activity": "Strike a Chord for Health," *NIH News in Health,* January 2010, https://tinyurl.com/t8jobpa.

Chapter 36

Page 135   "The annals of photography": Hanya Yanagihara, "Loneliness Belongs to the Photographer," *New Yorker*, July 10, 2016, https://tinyurl.com/vqjlula.

Chapter 37

Page 137   "For a long while Joan has managed to balance": Gin Phillips, *Fierce Kingdom* (New York: Viking, 2017), 1.

Page 140   "Finally we sit in the big bed": Lydia Kiesling, *The Golden State: A Novel* (New York: MCD Books, 2018), 22–23.

Chapter 38

Page 144   "*visio divina* invites one to encounter the divine": "Visio Divina," The Upper Room, https://tinyurl.com /vkx537s.

Chapter 39

Page 150   "like exuberant anger": Michaeleen Doucleff, "Got Anger? Try Naming It to Tame It," National Public Radio, January 28, 2019, https://tinyurl.com /ybd2edyb.

Chapter 41

Page 158   "the distinct peace that includes": This definition is adapted from Nicholas Paul Wolterstorff's definition from *Until Justice and Peace Embrace* (Grand Rapids: Eerdmans, 1983), 69–70.

Page 159   "When we express our longing": Kelly M. Kapic, *Embodied Hope: A Theological Meditation on Pain and Suffering* (Downers Grove, IL: IVP Academic, 2017), 29, 128.

Chapter 42

Page 161   "Just as physical pain protects people": Karyn Hall, "Accepting Loneliness," *Psychology Today*, January 13, 2013, https://tinyurl.com/stnjrkc.